Future

Anterior

Future Anterior
Volume XX, Numbers 1–2
Summer / Winter 2023

In This Issue

Report from Nisyros: Microhistories of a Thermal Bath Building in the Aegean Sea
Lydia Xynogala

This article examines a historic bath building and hotel in the Aegean Sea, the only one of its type still functioning. With the building currently under threat of an extensive, intrusive renovation, the text tackles different temporalities: those of bodies, building, landscape, and finally material as they related to time. Methodologically, the text draws from fieldwork, archival research, workshops organized with various age groups and local political agents, together with university students and faculty aiming in discussing the past, present and potential futures of this site. It is accompanied by the lens of an artist and photographer who joined the author in the workshop, drawings of children and oral histories of maintenance staff who worked there in the past, scans of its surfaces and dreams the author collected. In light of the threating alteration of its character, these different voices and formats of documenting one specific built heritage aim to address the question: how do we take care of buildings that are built to take care?

Conserving the Uncollectable? Museum Exhibitions and Preservation Advocacy, 1942–1980
Barry Bergdoll and Léa-Catherine Szacka

In 1975, New York's Museum of Modern Art (MoMA) staged the instantly infamous exhibition The Architecture of the Ecole des Beaux-Arts, generally associated with Arthur Drexler's seeming turn away from the museum's three decades of advocacy for modernism, and to his inadvertent opening to postmodernism. The conscious set of overlapping aims was to offer a critique of urban renewal, via a celebration of the so-called Beaux-Arts city, and—what is too rarely acknowledged—to advocate for preservation, in the wake of the loss of New York's Pennsylvania Station a decade earlier.

Museums played a significant role from their earliest history in preservation of architecture whole or in fragment, but the role of exhibitions in advocacy awaits its historian. From the late nineteenth-century open-air museums saved buildings by moving them into new plein-air settings; and the fashion for period rooms extended the notion of a collectible fragment to a component space of a disappeared architecture. But after

Future Anterior
Volume XX, Numbers 1–2
Summer / Winter 2023

World War II a new chapter in historic preservation opened with museological advocacy for the preservation in situ—outside the galleries of the museum—of nineteenth- and twentieth-century architecture and urban fabric. In recent years much has been written about the history of the preservation movement and, a veritable flood of studies has looked at the history of exhibitions. Yet the intersection of these two histories has received scant attention. This essay argues that a series of major institutions (notably New York's Museum of Modern Art, the Victoria & Albert Museum in London and, from the 1970s, the Venice Biennale) played an important role in municipal and national preservation of nineteenth- and early twentieth-century architecture, a forerunner in ways of the efforts of groups such as Docomomo in recent years.

The Abolitionist Landscape Project
Jeffrey Hogrefe

The "Abolitionist Landscape" is a geographic, geological, and social construction in the uplands of the states of Maryland, West Virginia, Virginia, and Pennsylvania where the events of the Indigenous diaspora and abolition of slavery played out on a big stage in the years leading up to the US Civil War. In this contested border, the US National Park Service maintains two monuments: Harpers Ferry National Monument, the site of John Brown's revolutionary act of 1859; and Antietam National Battlefield, the site of the 1862 battle that led to the Emancipation Proclamation of January 1, 1863, which issued freedom to over three million enslaved persons. The Indigenous and African voices that underlie the monuments and the rivers have been essentially silenced as a result of revisionist histories. This has had the effect of freezing past events in crystalline moments that privilege the Universalist image of the white soldier and white slave owning townspeople in a simulacrum. The article proposes that the human capacity to monumentalize that is supported by capital formations in the battlefields and historic towns of the Civil War can be acted on and against by the human capacity to locate interpretive practices that focus on the landscape as the singular origin of all meanings and walkers as co-creators of the landscape. A slow movement in, through and around the monuments locates, through sense-based walking practices in Afrosurrealism, an archive of historical documents, maps, and critical ethnography in response to the white supremacist historic preservation by the US National Park Service. The presentation of the events, objects and processional experiences propose a utopian future which repositions Blackness and Indigeneity as central to the landscape of the United States.

From Past to Future: The Walking Phenomenon in the Identity of Partizánske/Baťovany

Nina Bartošová, Barbora Vacková, and Veronika Rypák Vaňo

Partizánske, originally Baťovany, is even now admired as Slovakia's first functionalist town. It was conceived on the theory of the ideal industrial Baťa company town. Baťa was a Moravian shoe manufacturer based in Zlín that in the 1930s built satellite towns in many countries, including the United States, as smaller versions of Zlín. In the second half of the twentieth century both new construction and interventions in typically Baťa architecture stifled the town's original aesthetic. Thus, Partizánske's historical roots are less apparent than in Zlín. This article points to the possible benefit of expanding traditional architectural history research to include phenomenology, as justified by both current theoretical approaches and the use of the sociological method of the focus group. This suggested the potential in the walking phenomenon to strengthen the Partizánske identity. Considering current urban design trends giving precedence to pedestrian movement, for Partizánske this is a crucial aspect of the original urban design, and an intangible value that could be promoted with relatively little dependence on political or land ownership issues. Walking, as an enhancement of being-in-the-world, can for Partizánske become not just something to tie together individual zones but also the past and future.

Walking as Infrastructural Practice: Provisioning in Sampson Wong's "When in Doubt"

Sony Devabhaktuni

The article considers heritage through the walking practice of the Hong Kong artist and urbanist Sampson Wong. Wong's YouTube video channel "When in doubt, take a walk" (2020–2023) appeared shortly after political contestation in 2019 and the global COVID pandemic transformed the landscape of the city. This period effectively cut Hong Kong off from the world, but also from the possibility of memorializing the affectively charged traumas of protests that marked sites throughout the territory. Wong's video walks become participatory meanders that refamiliarize a city that had been closed to gathering and recollection. The article considers earlier theorizations of walking and the city and argues that "When in Doubt" can best be understood as both an *infrastructural practice* and a *practice of infrastructure*. This analysis brings together infrastructure's role as both a material and social mediation. The author draws on Lauren Berlant's work to consider how "When in Doubt" negotiates both the difficulty of holding on to attachments to the city and the notion of an easily shared, agreed-upon common. This reading extends understandings of heritage toward the productive ambivalences and loss that are central to the carrying through of the past into the present.

Heritage Imagination as a Spatial Practice, and the Possibility of Alternative Futures
Visa Immonen

In heritage scholarship, imagination appears to create something novel and positive, but the term itself, along with the related noun "imaginary" and verb "to imagine" are rarely discussed at length. This article, examines imagination through the concept of "heritage imagination." Heritage imagination is based on our experiences of heritage, which form a basis for further disciplinary analysis. Heritage imagination contains a supposition that knowledge produced by Heritage Studies can ultimately be employed to improve human existence. Philosophical debate on imagination shows that it is not only epistemological, affecting how we perceive and think, but also ontological, referring to embodied ways in which we live in the world. Although heritage imagination comes with a promise of alternative futures, all imaginings do not produce great transformations, but rather form a routine part of living one's life. Hence, attaining alternative heritage futures might not so much require the formation of seemingly new and untamed visions as the clearing of space for thinking and the conception of indeterminate futures.

Mind the Gap: Experimenting with Circularity in Built Environment through The Restoration Toolbox
Aishwarya Tipnis

As one of the world's fastest growing economies, with a stupendously high rate of urbanization, Indian cities are further plagued by the climate crisis. The direct impact is on the built and natural heritage of our cities. Hapless destruction, large-scale demolitions and massive constructions not only have led to the cities losing their individuality but also have caused severe environmental degradation, high levels of pollution, and construction waste. As the third largest emitter globally, India's decarbonization policy aims at achieving net zero by 2070. The key strategies proposed are adopting green hydrogen, carbon capture usage and storage (CCUS), natural climate solutions and material circularity. Although restoring and reusing heritage buildings has been recognized as a key strategy contributing to the circular economy, the on-ground situation in India tells another story. Based on learnings from practice, the key challenge in changing existing mindsets, where the preference lies in new build rather than reuse. This article presents the

Figure 1. Baths and rooms lined up along the corridor. An interplay of sleeping, bathing, socializing. Photo credit: Tobias Wootton.

Lydia Xynogala

Report from Nisyros
Microhistories of a Thermal Bath Building in the Aegean Sea

Loutra (Baths), Nisyros, The Dodecanese, Greece

The smell of sulfur is mixed with that of the sea; I can hear the sounds of the waves a few meters away, coming through the windows. Inside the building, behind closed doors, thermal water flows and echoes down a long corridor. Gazing up, the high ceiling's strong blue oil paint guides you along, and the generous width of the space turn this passage into a promenade (Figure 1). Colored ceramic floor tiles in geometric shapes complement this visual journey: This long corridor is not just a means of connection, a route to reach a destination, but rather a communal space where one wants to linger. At the entry hallway a round, broad, wood-carved stair leads to the foyer of the second floor. Shuffling sounds of footsteps from the identical corridor upstairs as the old timber floorboards respond to weight and movement. The passage down the corridor is a constant reminder of the space's relationship with two water bodies, the Mediterranean Sea outside, and the thermal spring inside. Their presence is felt and gives directions to the eye and to the body: how to move, walk, gaze, and rest.

Building Chemistry

On the southern side of the corridor, doors lead me into the thermal baths. There, eleven partitioned rooms in a light green hue are each fitted with a rectangular marble tub. Inside, the water contains hydro-sulfur mixed with salt water and is pumped in from the nearby source: the baths are situated where the thermal spring emerges. This chemistry gives the water, the building, and the bodies a smell, drawing us to the volcanic crater on the mountain up above. Geothermal fluids connect the architecture to the volcano, transporting its mineral consistency as hydrogen sulfide finds its way into sea water. Because of these fluid dynamics, hot water—which is lighter than the cooler sea water—accumulates under island rocks. It then finds its way onto the surface, spurting out at the coast, floating above the saline water.[1] With a temperature of 46°C, it flows straight into the tubs where it can be cooled down as per the bathers' preference. Hydrogen Sulfide, H_2S, penetrates the skin and mucosae, treating disorders of the internal organs—high blood pressure, ischemia, and kidney conditions—and generally calms the nervous system.[2] There is no clock in this small room with the tub, but you will hear a

Future Anterior
Volume XX, Numbers 1–2
Summer / Winter 2023

voice calling you to end your bath; one can only stay fifteen to twenty minutes in the water. Bathing for longer weakens you, bringing the opposite to the desired effect. During this time of immersion, the body begins to float as the salt makes the water buoyant. In this measured time, one is left to observe the changing shadows, light and sounds; echoes of waterdrops from the adjoining rooms.[3]

Once the bath has ended, I walk down the corridor to return to my room. Positioned along its north side, are a series of adjacent spaces overlooking the sea. In plan, the rooms are small, fitted with the bare essentials: a window, bed, sink, desk, chair, and closet. One doesn't however feel confined in this small room; the tall ceilings and openness to the sea horizon give space in other ways. Contemplating the sea from the window, I see the faint silhouette of the Turkish coast, a mere twenty kilometers away. Almost equidistant from here and to the Datça peninsula is the invisible maritime border between Greece and Turkey. In the past, this border was crisscrossed with boats from the coast to this island but today this open naval traffic exchange has greatly diminished (Figure 2).[4]

Loutra (which means "baths" in Greek) is the building's location in the island of Nisyros and takes its name from the thermal bath complex. Loutra forms a healing triangle with two other geographical points, one in Turkey, the other in Greece. On one side of the border, in Turkey's Asia Minor, is Knidos, the ancient city and medical school. On the other side, twenty-five kilometers north of Loutra is the Asclepeion and Hippocratic center for medicine on the neighboring Greek island of Kos. These two ancient schools of medicine represented radically different approaches to healing.[5]

To the northwest, I see another figure in the sea: Gyali is a small island next to Nisyros and under continuous extraction. At the top of a soft white sculpted landscape bulldozers push pumice stone. It falls into shifters, conveyor belts and loaded onto large boats that dock nearby. I think of this simultaneous extraction of minerals: here in this building, minerals enter the body coming from the spring, which derives from the volcano. Across in Gyali, mineral matter, pumice stone is loaded on boats which then take it to the US, Israel, and elsewhere.[6] In Antiquity, obsidian, a sharp, black, shiny stone used for making tools, weapons, and mirrors was also mined here.

Climbing the topography—south of Loutra—the Stefanos, Alexandros, and Polyvotis craters form a yellow sulfurous terrain. An active volcano, from 1871 to 1873 the island experienced a series of eruptions, and two new craters were formed. In the last eruption of 1887, mud, rocks and steam emissions were recorded.[7] To this day, the presence of steam can be observed throughout the island: released in the form

Figure 2. Rooms and smaller corridors overlook into the sea. Far in the horizon the Turkish coast is visible. Photo credit: Tobias Wootton.

of fumaroles in the crater, occasionally puncturing the soil and emerging from the terrain or within buildings. Oral histories of Loutra speak of the existence of a *ksefisistra,* a hole where steam from the volcano emerged within the building. In the past, bathers could also perform inhalation therapies, breathing, in a way, into the building. Water and steam thus become the other building matter, essential for producing its unique atmosphere. Other patients would dilute the sulfurous volcanic soil into the thermal waters, to heal illnesses of the skin, such as psoriasis.

Hot springs appear where regional tectonic faults intersect with radial volcanic faults[8]; they are at points of ground ruptures. One such point is Loutra. While the tectonic qualities of the ground are those of a rupture, the bath building fosters closeness and sociability. Both ground and second floors have generous common spaces with bays of large windows, a library, seating area and large table; they foster the spirit of communal gatherings. Moments of surprise punctuate the rhythm of adjacent rooms along the corridors. At one turn, a small stair and landing lead you to a window overlooking a temple outside. Another single window interrupts the rhythm of rooms and offers an unexpected view of the sea.

Figure 3. Bath building complex: Left to right, Class A (still operating), Class B, and Class C (shut). Photo credit: Tobias Wootton.

I walk outside and toward the sheltered marina to get an overview. There are three buildings, the one just described and two others next to it, currently abandoned and in poor shape (Figure 3).[9]

Building, Island Histories

The construction history of these baths dates back to 1870 when, in this location a Nisyrian built a room with three tubs to heal his skin ailment. The healing properties of the water drew the interest of the community, and he later donated the room to the municipality. A series of loans provided by prominent local residents and an increased community interest led to the construction of the first building in 1885.[10] The "Kalisperis" building was named after one of the main advocates for its construction. This building had seven rooms and seven tubs. Later, four more rooms were added. In 1894 it was decided to create a new two-floor building designed by an engineer of the Prefecture of Rhodes,[11] with twelve tubs, eight rooms, and a balcony on the upper floor. What enabled the completion of this wing was a donation from the Nisyrian Society of New York, Porfyris. The building was named "aristocratic" or porfyric,[12] alluding to the production of the precious dye in Antiquity: among a string of other Aegean islands, Nisyros was key in the production of this purple color and the ancient name of the island was Porfyris. The Phoenicians "mined" the sea here for the special murex shells to acquire the purple color and dye precious textiles. Extraction of the geophysical matter of the island continued in the early twentieth century: Greek business interests were aware of the rich-in sulfur soil which the Ottomans used for decades to manufacture gunpowder. Further, according to a French writer: "The English colonizers, always zealous, had planted their flag there, in the hope of establishing a coal depot on the island. Projects quickly swallowed [it] up. And we agree that this close and unfortunate example is not made to encourage long-term speculation in Nisyros."[13]

But there was plenty of speculation, sparked further by the Greek businessman Alexandros Ralli, whose sulfur enterprise was received joyously by the island. He built a sulfur factory bringing the soil directly from the volcano's crater into the Agia Irini cove for further processing.[14] South from the crater, the sulfur bath complex comprised a total of three buildings with ninety-seven rooms, each catering to a different clientele: first-class patrons; second- and third- class rooms where low-income patients could stay and receive treatment, often times free of charge. A direct boat connection was established from Nisyros to Egypt, bringing in patients, predominantly Greeks of the Diaspora, to take the waters. When the Italian colonization of the Dodecanese begun in 1912, the island witnessed a gradual increase in controls from the Italian authorities. These concerned all aspects of civic life[15] and brought a halt to this healing movement: boat traffic from Egypt was banned and the great loss of profits resulted in the slow demise and closure of the entire complex under the Italian regime. From 1936 to 1962, a guard and maintenance person were installed to safeguard the building and make sure the baths were safe from looting.

In 1942, amidst the war, the building assumed another caring role: the Italian authorities converted it into an orphanage for children from across the Dodecanese Island complex. One hundred orphans found refuge in the baths accompanied by *frerides,* Catholic priests. The first-class salon was converted into a church, while other common spaces were turned into a school. At the end of World War II, the municipality decided to reopen the baths, this time with their original program. Another large grant by New York–based Nisyrians, this time the Gnomagoras Society, allowed for the baths' reopening in the summer of 1948.[16] Nisyros saw a large wave of its people immigrating to the US and Australia during the interwar and postwar eras. The various regimes, from the Ottoman Empire to Italian colony, then war, brought hardships and poverty; the large number of Nisyrian immigrants established a prosperous community in New York and published a number of journals, including Gnomagoras, to record the history and traditions of the island. These journals, with subscriptions from Nisyrians around the world, allowed the community of ex-pats to remain connected and engaged in local affairs. Of tantamount importance on a local level was the fate of the baths, which, as extensively documented in these publications, had become the pride of the Nisyrian community. A string of loans and donations from Nisyrians abroad for repair and maintenance works kept the buildings functioning for decades.

These attempts by the New York Nisyrian community to preserve the baths took place alongside political efforts from the same community to secure Dodecanese's independence and induction into the Greek State.[17] In 1912 a Dodecanese referendum expressed the wish of the islands to be unified with Greece, in the previous century, they had fought in the war against the Ottoman Empire (1821–29) in support of the Greek independence. In 1935, 10,000 copies of the publication titled "The Unredeemed Islands of Greece," a text authored by the Dodecanesian Youth of the United States, were widely distributed, reaching the United States president among numerous other North American and international state officials.[18] But the twelve-island complex was only incorporated into Greece in 1948 and started to participate in its political life in 1950, when the Dodecanese citizens could, for the first time, participate in parliamentary elections. In 1951, a book by the Nisyrian Iakovos Kazavis, published in New York,[19] quotes Walt Whitman in introducing the islands' struggle for independence, and the role of the preservation of memory in ideas towards freedom.[20]

When the baths resumed operations in 1948, a doctor was present every day to cater to the incoming patients, but accommodation was challenging: a lack of running water, fridge, and provision of meals, made the patients' stay uncomfortable.[21] Slow changes and improvements were introduced by the installation of the electricity grid in Nisyros and a restaurant opened in the first-class building. Operations continued until 1990, when the municipality decided to remove the roofs of the second- and third-class buildings, which they deemed dangerous, and to restore them. This renovation was never completed, and ruination ensued as the buildings lacked roofs and were exposed to the harsh weather of the sea. Recently, in the summer of 2021, another New Yorker Nisyrian made a generous donation with the goal to restore the entire complex.

Generosity and Care

Generosity is the generative factor of the bath's construction history, from its founding as a small bath to its expansion into a complex of three buildings. This generosity and care are manifest in its architecture (Figure 4). The long corridor, the common rooms on each floor, the restaurant at the other end, a shared balcony, a terrace. A similar layout is repeated on the second level, although there are no baths on this floor. A sec-

Figure 4. Rooms are small but common areas in both two floors are generous. These spaces become meeting points, allow for intimate or larger gatherings. Photo credit: Tobias Wootton.

ond set of rooms overlooks the volcanic terrain in the back. Two spacious common rooms on both floors interrupt the sequence of hotel rooms overlooking the sea. This generous arrangement of private and public spaces allows the visitor to experience moments of solitude and togetherness.

Though I had previously stayed in the baths, I returned in October 2021, as part of a group of forty students, teaching members, and artists, for a seminar week.[22] We experienced the generosity and care that characterize this place. From conversations in the communal spaces on both floors, to brief words in the corridor, solitary experiences in the baths, morning and night swims, care from those who run it, and more conversations, debates, thoughts and questions, flowed through the building.

The mayor of Nisyros presented us his vision for the island: a "zero-waste" Nisyros. We inquired about the future of this building and the renovation plans funded by the recent donation. The municipality would match the donation the mayor explained, with the goal to restore the entire bath complex of all three buildings. He stressed that the corridors would remain intact, but rooms would change to accommodate private bathrooms. The municipality also planned to turn the two ruined buildings into accommodation with en-suite bathrooms, necessitating a substantial renovation would have to take place given their current state. Any interior layout changes would gravely impact the historic character of this site. In the still-functioning building, renovation works should be limited to structural and restorative interventions. Greece has a large number of thermal bath infrastructures: a 1938 publication titled "The 750 Mineral Springs of Greece"[23] lists them all while several more were built in the 1950s. The surviving baths are a trace of movement that has its origins in mid-nineteenth-century Greece, with peaks in the interwar and postwar era. During these times bath buildings were constructed throughout the country; today the majority is in poor shape or completely abandoned, with few exceptions. An even smaller number of bath hotels exists in their original state. The popular Thermae Sylla in Aidipsos has been renovated beyond recognition of its interior. Sarlitza Pallas in Lesvos Island and the baths in Kythnos Island, which were built by the Bavarian King Otto have been abandoned for decades. The hotel Ai Pigai in Methana is still operating but with substantial renovations that have removed their historic details and character.

The Loutra in Nisyros is the only surviving and functioning thermal bath hotel in Greece with its original interior intact: an important landmark of cultural heritage not just for Greece, but for the Mediterranean region. It also stands as a memorial for the days when invisible nautical borders were not in place, when free marine traffic from Africa, Turkey, and Europe brought patients to this small island. A locus of healing, care and generosity; a reminder of times when community efforts achieved works for the public good. It is in danger to be sacrificed in the name of luxury, extra comfort, the "tourist prospects" coupled with short sighted local politics of reelection.

Reenactments

I found postcards from the 1920s that depict the rival bath hotel of the island, in Pallous, now abandoned (Figure 5).[24] One scene is particularly striking whereby the bath owner staged a demonstration of a dance in the bath's salon, an attempt to bind ancient Greek history with Nisyros. The women wear ancient Greek-like white dresses, with meanders at the hem and featuring behind them, the mural of a temple. The caption reads:

> The ancient Hellenic dance with the ancient costume of the Caryatides in the large hall of the theater of the ancient Hippocrates thermal springs of Dr. Pantelidis in Palous Nisyros.

At the time these postcards were printed,[25] Nisyros was not part of the Greek State. We reenact the postcard with the students in the main hall of the baths in *Loutra* as the salon space is a close match to the one from the photograph.

Figure 5. The legacy of Hippocrates, who practiced in nearby Kos and brought his patients to bathe in Nisyros, carried on in the promotional material of the rival, privately owned bath building, as an attempt to bind ancient Greek past at a time of still Ottoman and then Italian occupation of the island.

Return

We return a year later from the first visit with ETH Zurich, Chair for the History of Art and Architecture in October 2022 (Figures 6 and 7). The local political representatives are advancing with their future "restoration" plans, and my goal is to create transparency in the process as no competition or study of the forthcoming works is made public. In an effort to create public awareness I organized two days of workshops: one for the elementary-school children and one for the high-school students. The majority have never set foot in the baths so I ask them to draw the building, select a space, a corner, a detail. To pay attention to one's aspect hometown's heritage, is an act of care. I further collected oral histories of those who worked there, as bath nurses, cooks, and maintenance staff.

Some children have never visited the baths before. Preservation is also the making of a collective memory:

> People only came only for baths. We had people coming continuously for forty years. I had a great time with them, I was loved too. People felt better, their health was much better. They had a better winter. Then they stopped coming, I don't know why. For us, the place is something important, we have springs, and we take our baths. We see a big difference in our health, joints, hands. For us it is a form of wealth, I think. The building could be in better condition. They have been trying for some years to do renovations, I don't know where they are stuck, what is the problem. All the elderly returning here every summer

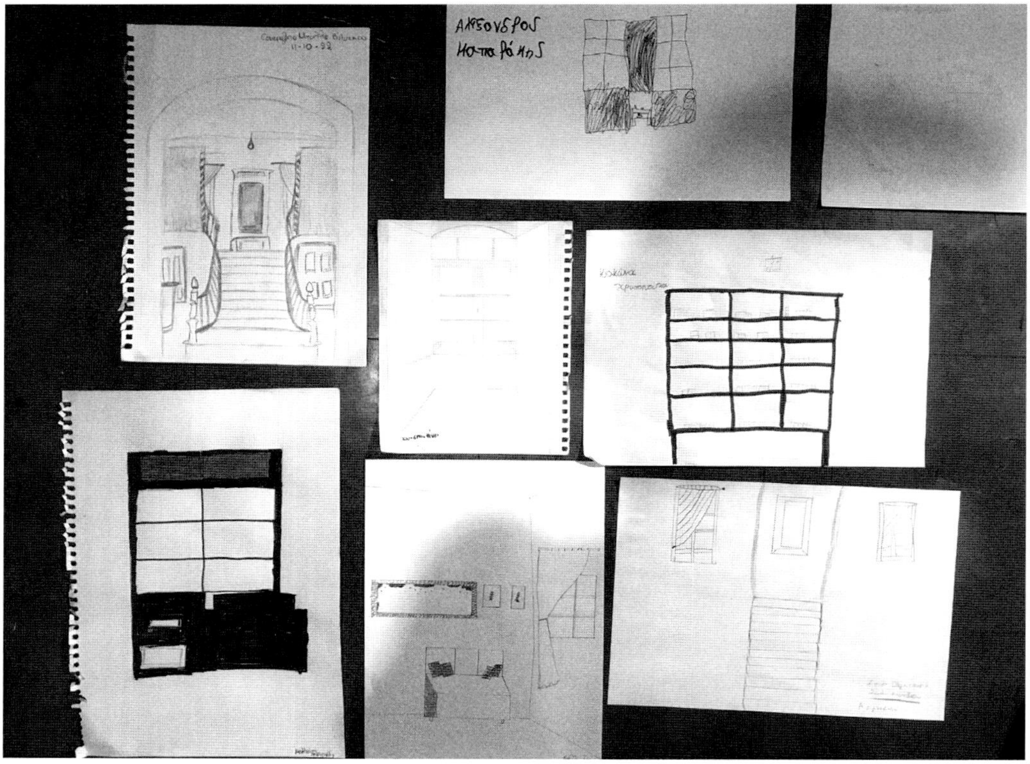

Figure 6. Primary and high-school children draw the building at a workshop organized in October 2022.

they would discuss how they spent their winter. They were happy to meet again and find each other every year, in the same place.

My father-in-law lived here and he had planted all these trees. I know of women who came here for years to have children and that this helped them a lot and in fact two girls came and baptized their children here on the island. One named [her child] after Panagia Thermiani. You can't describe the building. Its healing water, its history make it unique."

—Z.K., maid at the baths thirty-one years ago

I had the kitchen for three years. These were the best years of my life. Before I had six children, I was isolated at home, in the 1960s, things were difficult. And when I went there, my house had been damaged by earthquakes and I was in trouble. I fed everyone [who visited]. There was chaos, a celebration. . . . I met a lot of nice people. Mostly poor and elderly, who came to take their baths from Rhodes, the villages of Archangelos, Kremasti, from Karpathos, from Kos from Athens.

The baths helped them a lot because they came every year, they saw a big difference. We had parties every night, fake weddings, engagements, proms, I made sweets. I worked in the baths, I didn't make any money, but I fed everybody. I had taken a big cassette player, and we danced. Women from Agios Isidoros were coming and they didn't want to leave. I cooked for them, and they cried and cried. A girl got up from the table, and we went looking for her. She was crying, I found her in her bed. "Why are you crying?" I asked? "I don't want to leave; I want to stay with you." "Stay," I told her. . . . I had a very nice time with them, I have a phone book and they still call me after all these years. If I had years ahead of me, I would like to still be there, working. I did it all by myself, I fed at least three hundred people a day. We roasted goats, made buffets. . . . The mayor asked me to be a cook for the bathers. My father died when I was a baby and my mother worked in the fields to raise us, so I cooked [for my family]. My mother was illiterate, but she was very intelligent, she knew all the jobs. And that's how I learned them too. . . . Now people don't come anymore, they cut off their social security. The waters helped those who could not walk, who had pain in their back, their legs.

—P.K., cook during the 1990s

At a very young age, I remember that in addition to the baths, they also did mud therapy. . . . This mud was carried from the volcano with donkeys, and there were only a few who performed this treatment. And they probably also had the corresponding disease. . . . My father was the keeper of the baths, simultaneously doing some maintenance when they were not working in both the interior and the exterior. What has made a lasting impression on me is the people who used to return, again, and again because they saw a significant improvement in their condition. And they brought others with them. It used to be a very good bath town. And I remember the locals liked to hear from the visitors, the patients who came, that they were happy. In other words, our waters had the substances that were important for certain ailments. . . . For me, the memories are very good, but I am already sad because we are not worthy successors of our ancestors and the baths remain in this state. I believe that we have both the financial capabilities and the knowledge to do it.

—L.K., whose father was the superintendent of the baths, and lived next door

I also collected dreams and impressions from the students with whom we visited the baths. I include one memory below:

My dream relationship with this bath hotel could probably best be indicated by the following episode. A few months later after our visit, I took part in a course to deal with the self-alienation. One time I was given an assignment—in a light trance I had to visualize the home of my dreams and describe it in as much spatial detail as possible. What came out was the Loutra Hotel. The large old table stood in the large guest room, the sea filtered through the old fine-sounding window frames from the front and the evening sunlight warmed through the large altar windows at the back. The architecture of the balcony framed the waves, the sky-colored dills shone, the old mirrors reflected the souls of friends. Apart from us, the house was populated by people coming and going, sharing their creativity and warmth, coming and going they gathered in the evenings in the large guest room. You might ask—what does this have to do with a private home? I didn't care at all. Your house of real nostalgia not calculated or staged doesn't have to be private at all. In Andrey Tarkovsky's Solaris, for example, it is a house from a Breughel painting. Such spaces cannot be artificially produced, they grow and age together with the place – with its rocks, trees and neighborhoods. They only need to be found—discovered—one day. . . .

—N.G.

Time

> The reader, at this point, will have realized for some time now that this is not a chemical treatise: my presumption does not reach so far—"ma voix est foible, et mime un peu profane." Nor is it an autobiography, save in the partial and symbolic limits in which every piece of writing is autobiographical, indeed every human work; but it is in some fashion a history. It is—or would have liked to be—a microhistory, the history of a trade and its defeats, victories, and miseries, such as everyone wants to tell when he feels close to concluding the arc of his career, and art ceases to be long.[26]
>
> —Primo Levi

The story of the baths through their protagonists, human and mineral, is a microhistory of the island. Writing is an attempt to record time and its changes; they are observed in the bodies, buildings, and geology that make up Nisyros. Recording these changes is also an act of preservation of otherwise forgotten intangible realities. The fifteen minutes spent in a bath in Loutra gives the body the time it needs to stock up on minerals, beyond which, they can become harmful to the organs. We are moving in time: from mineralization in the body, to mineralization of the earth. As a volcano emerged from the sea 150,000 years ago, its eruptions and aggregation of ash and lava slowly created a conical land shape. Molten rock, eruption upon eruption, gave shape to Nisyros and the nearby Gyali. Here time has another visible dimension as the two ends of Gyali island, visible from the baths, are moving one centimeter closer together every year by, the mining engineer told me.

In the marble tubs of Loutra, patients would submerge in sulfurous water. For the first couple of days of treatment, hydro sulfur makes your head heavy. You can even have visions of a spectrum of colors at night. Mineralization begins. Sulfur builds up in the body. Organs, bones, tissue start absorbing the minerals. "Hydrogen sulfide is produced by the decomposition of various mineral sulphates in the water,[27] through the synergy of plant substances. These have been mixed in the layers of the earth, through which the waters pass through before gushing out."[28] Plant life aids mineral life, which then enters human bodies. Life, to non-life, and back to life. Sulfur is bound with the material and oral histories of Nisyros. Some, like Jeancard, travelled to see the volcano, while others came to take care of their bodies: arthritis, skin issues, infertility.[29] Parents would return to Nisyros with the child they had after receiving treatment there.

Sulfur is what Aristotle may have called άφθαρτη ουσία, an incorruptible, primary substance.[30] In Nisyros, sulfur and its by-products in water and soil became the matter of care and also of the island's livelihood. As one voice from 1842 recounts, the abundance of sulfur was first used as an exported matter: "It is considered particularly lucky for the island if every two or three years a caique appears to take a load of sulfur."[31] The island's geologic, volcanic, eruptive, healing, fertile matter remains been the focus to this day, the driver for this small geography's growth. When the extraction business closed down, the baths remained the hope for the island's development.

> The absence of a significant income from the exploitation of the sulfur for years is sufficiently noticeable that the Nisyrians wait anxiously, but always with reverent patience and determination, to improve the situation with a new era of exploitation of the sulfur and from the long recognition of the extraordinary healing properties of the hot springs, the antiquities, the natural beauty, and the geological wonders of their beautiful mysterious homeland, which are going to draw endless groups of enthusiastic healthy visitors and patients as the majority of the future and departure healthy.[32]

The island turned its gaze from extraction and focused on healing. However, the gaze returned back to extraction in the postwar era through its neighboring island Yali.[33] The pumice deposits there will be exhausted by 2100. And we arrive to today, where the gaze is turning back into intensifying the exploitation of the baths, this time with a different clientele in mind, to align with the predominant narrative of luxury tourism, widespread in Greece of today. Yet, this focus once again fosters a "monoculture" of sorts. Efforts of privatizations which already begun at the dawn of the Greek financial crisis of 2008, intensified in the post-COVID landscape, with Greece adopting the global trends of a "wellness culture" in par with tourism for the elites.[34] To paying close attention to this building's history is also to imagine its potential futures, away from the narratives of luxury SPA exploitation and fast tourism consumption. A preservation effort should allow for these sites of care to remain open to all. Thus, interventions must allow for the diversity of micro-histories to continue to unfold. How do we take care of buildings that are built to take care? Recording material changes, stories of healing and togetherness has been the first step towards building an archive of knowledge about this place.

In built matters: Currently, during the summer, because of its low cost the baths attract a young clientele, often musicians who also perform and record in the space, appreciating its acoustics; while September is an optimal month for mineral spring bathing for senior patients. In former times, the three different buildings with their respective amenities allowed for visitors of vastly different incomes. A similar approach could be adopted today. The adjacent buildings can be carefully renovated to accommodate different accommodation needs and respectively generate a diverse range of visitors and income for the municipality. A thermal pool that is currently envisioned should be carefully considered: oftentimes abusing a thermal source's capacity of daily water can lead to its exhaustion.

The still-functioning building requires a careful approach: The bathrooms can continue to be a shared amenity, and therefore maintain its affordability. Two rooms facing the back, can be turned into additional communal bathrooms. Elements that are greatly impacted by the sea need to be cared for: restoring the timber floor and replacing the timber windows with double glazing. This would also allow for the building, which currently has no heating, to be used for a longer period of time; the island has a short winter. Currently, the baths close in early October and only reopen for the public in June, sometimes opening up just for the local residents. Extending thus the season from March to November, will allow for a new programing, uses, more patients and diverse clientele through the seasons.

Figure 7. Workshop with ETH Zurich, Chair of the History of Art and Architecture, Prof. Dr. Philip Ursprung, with the Municipal Representatives of Nisyros, at Loutra, October 2022. On the wall, drawings made of the building by the children of Nisyros, in a workshop organized by the author.

Yet, these efforts must be protected through legislation: while the building's exterior is considered "historic," it's interior and broader landscape of the site, is not protected by law. Already in 1919, legislation,[35] advocated by the chemist, professor and advocate of the healing waters of Greece, Anastasios Dambergis proposed the declaration of thermal springs as public assets, dedicated to healing the community. It would be worth revisiting this idea, expressed a century ago.

The rich history of this building reveals the unique layering of volcanic matter, bodies, sites, buildings; they coexist as different temporalities in Nisyros. Geological time in the form of eruptions and disruptions; aching, aging bodies returning every year to the baths; historic time and regimes manifest in the built typologies and fragments found on the ground; community efforts throughout history, a building that ages in need of conservation. I attempt to write architectural history through its mineral layers because I find matter inseparable from the buildings, landscapes, bodies and communities it affected. If we consider the mineral as agent of transformation, then we can move through time and scale.

Restoring the Body, Restoring the Building

Architecture is a material practice unfolding in time; here in the baths, spaces negotiate temporalities of individuals, of communities, of regimes. I express the hope that the current maintenance effort will conserve and pay attention to all these temporalities. Elizabeth Povinelli writes:"Rather than focusing on the difference between Life and Nonlife . . . let's rethink the link between the geochemistry of Earth and the biochemistry of Life."[36] In this building's history, the link are the minerals; they are part of a narrative that engages corporeal architecture, history, and the site's potentiality. Preservation of this heritage is thus the collective memory of bodies, buildings and landscapes. The anthropologist Anna Tsing speaks of third natures, what manages to live despite capitalism.[37] Recording time through minerals embodies a sense of duration, one where temporality of matter is relative to the temporality of corporeal care. In this site, the building and its natures have endured, until now.[38]

The healing legacy of Nisyros—echoing that of the nearby Asklepion—and the incorporation of sulphur baths into contemporary health practices may seem sensible at first glance. However, it is necessary to consider a broader conception of the "health/care" narrative—one that transcends superficial associations. This requires an approach rooted in a deeper understanding of well-being—one that embraces the essence of the place, harnessing somewhat fragmented yet personal memories and imagery: Nisyros, in dialogue with its residents, its built and intangible heritage, and beyond. To establish a common purpose, preservation efforts must attune to rituals of drawing, sensing, and listening—to humans and more-than-humans, to minerals and buildings, to communities and individuals alike.

Biography
Lydia Xynogala is an architect and post-doc fellow at Accademia di Architettura in Mendrisio and at Karlsruhe University of Arts and Design. Her doctoral dissertation at the gta Institute, ETH Zurich, examined the construction of a culture centered around natural resources in twentieth-century Greece and has been nominated for the ETH Medal. Her architectural practice, ALOS, and research engage built artifacts and their material effects within environmental histories and cultural narratives and has been exhibited at Storefront, LMAK Gallery NY, AIA Center for Architecture NY and gta exhibitions in Zurich. She holds degrees from Princeton University, Cooper Union, and the Bartlett. Previously she taught at ETH Zurich, Columbia GSAPP, The Cooper Union, RPI, and CCNY New York. Her work has been supported with grants by the New York Foundation for the Arts, the Onassis Foundation, and the Greek Architecture Award for best built work. She is founder of the nonprofit association "Friends of the 750 Mineral Springs of Greece" and curator of the exhibition "Loutropolis."

Acknowledgments
My deep gratitude to Philip Ursprung and the Chair for the History of Art and Architecture at ETH Zurich for continuing support in this project and for all the input in the conference conducted with the Mayor of Nisyros. I thank my colleagues from ETH Zurich, Nina Zschocke and Tim Klauser, who joined me onsite for the conference. Further generous input then was provided by Aristede Antonas, Adam Jasper, and Tobias Wootton, who contributed with his photography of the buildings. Takis Andriotis and Apostolis Mastroyiannis provided great onsite support for this research on a number of occasions.

Notes

[1] Georgios Vougioukalakis, *Nisyros Volcano,* pdf report, GME (Greek Institute of Geology & Mineral Exploration), 40. I thank the author for sharing this report with me.

[2] Jose Manuel Carbajo and Francisco Maraver, "Sulphurous Mineral Waters: New Applications for Health," *Evidence-Based Complementary and Alternative Medicine: ECAM* 2017 (2017): 8034084.

[3] To quote Carlo Ginzburg, this text is looking at "themes that have been previously ignored or relegated to spheres considered inferior such as local history." Carlo Ginzburg, John Tedeschi, and Anne C. Tedeschi, "Microhistory: Two or Three Things That I Know about It," *Critical Inquiry* 20, no. 1 (1993): 10–35, 32. Fieldwork and research were generated in the framework of my ongoing doctoral dissertation at the gta Institute, ETH Zurich, on the construction of a culture of care centered around natural resources in twentieth-century Greece, in focus are the bath buildings and mineral springs as sites for healing. On the history of this healing movement through thermal waters, see Lydia Xynogala, "On Airs, Waters and Places: The Construction of Natural History of Healthcare," in *Social Distance*, gta Papers 5, ed. Adam Jasper (Zürich: gta Verlag, 2021).

[4] During the summer months there are ferries connecting Kos to Bodrum and Marmaris to Kos. There is no direct boat from Turkey to Nisyros.

[5] Knidian medical practitioners were interested in the "local" character of disease, studying the illness itself. The Hippocratic school was invested in its "general" character, eighteen focusing on the individual person. See Mehmet Turgut, "Ancient Medical Schools in Knidos and Kos," *Child's Nervous System* 27, no. 2 (February 2011): 197–200.

[6] On the history of mineral exploitation in Greece and a description of the island of Gyali, see also Lydia Xynogala, "Mineral Travels: Fragments of Geographies on the Move," in *Bodies of Extraction: Underneath the Grounjd of Islands* (Athens: Kyklàda Press, 2022).

[7] Johannes C. Hunziker, *The Geology, Geochemistry and Evolution of Nisyros Volcano (Greece): Implications for the Volcanic Hazards*, Vol. 44 Mémoires de Géologie (Lausanne) (Lausanne: Section des Sciences de la Terre, Université de Lausanne, 2005).

[8] Volker Jörg Dietrich, Evangelos Lagios, and Springer International Publishing, *Nisyros Volcano the Kos—Yali—Nisyros Volcanic Field* (Berlin: Springer, 2018), 171.

[9] Yiorgos Tsironis, *Technical Report of Loutra*. March 2015 (unpublished). Commissioned study to maintain and restore the bath buildings, the report was shared with me by the managing company of the baths *Ditouren*.

[10] For a detailed description of the construction history, see Yiannis Chartofilis, *Natroclorioucha Iamatika Loutra Dimou Mandrakiou Nisyrou*, Athens 2013, 9–12 (Saline Healing Baths of the Mandraki Municipality).

[11] Charles Flegel, *Asia Minor Baths, Nisyros Island and Its Thermal Springs* (1899; repr. Athens: Sakoula Publishers, 2007), 42.

[12] Flegel, *Asia Minor Baths*, 15.

[13] Paul Jeancard, *L'Anatolie* (Paris: Librairie Francaise 1919), 135. In this book, Jeancard details his travels in Smyrne, Sparta, Bourdour, Hierapolis, and the Dodecanse. The chapter on Nisyros begins with his ascent to the volcano. On the way there he looks over at the roofs of the baths.

[14] The Rallis Brothers were a powerful merchant family with business in London, factories in India, and world trading operations. See Vikram Doctor, "Ralli Brothers: The History Remains as a Reminder of Entrepreneurial Abilities of Economically Shattered Greeks," *The Economic Times*, August 2, 2015, https://economictimes.indiatimes.com/magazines/panache/ralli-brothers-the-history-remains-as-a-reminder-of-entrepreneurial-abilities-of-economically-shattered-greeks/articleshow/48311628.cms.

[15] The effects of Italian colonization in the Dodecanese region are described in detail in Nicholas Doumanis, "Dodecanese Islands," in *A Historical Companion to Postcolonial Literatures: Continental Europe and Its Empires*, ed. Poddar Prem et al. (Edinburgh: Edinburgh University Press, 2008), 276–77. See also Nicholas Doumanis, "Italy's Aegean Possession: The Dodecanese Islands, 1912–47," in *Myth and Memory in the Mediterranean* (London: Macmillan, 1997).

[16] Kōstas E. Mantoudakēs, *Nisyros Kai Nisyrioi* [Nisyros and Nisyrians] (Athens: Em. Rodakē, 1979).

[17] Iakovos Kazavis, *Dodekanisiakai Energeiai* [Dodecanesian actions] (New York: Cosmos Greek–American Printing Company, 1951).

[18] In a paragraph titled "In America" Kazavis refers to a memorandum printed in New York that advocated for freedom, published in 10,000 copies and distributed in embassies and numerous governments. The text in both Greek and English lists how the booklet was distributed "to the United States President, to the fifty six ambassadors from different nations stationed in Washington, to the ninety six senators of the United States Senate, to the four leading political parties of the United States . . . to the twenty eight members of the British Cabinet in London, to the twenty one judges of the Permanent Court of International Justice in Hague, to the fifty seven Ambassadors from the United States to different capitals of the world," among many others. Kazavis, *Dodekanisiakai Energeiai*, 76.

[19] The text by Kazavis refers to an earlier publication in the *Dodecanesion Journal* of New York, in 1937, which advocates for the liberation of the island complex.

[20] Kazavis, *Dodekanisiakai Energeiai*, 23.
[21] The EOT internal report published in 1951, authored by Andreas Iatridis, describes the dire condition of the building following the war. This report was found in the personal archives of Eugenios Fokas, and records the first statistics of bathers, with one table specially dedicated to baths taken free of charge or at a discount. Nisyros, now a part of the Greek State, is within the statistics. According to it in the period 1950–51, the baths in Nisyros had 44 bathers with 557 baths taken in total. In comparison, Kythnos had 22 and 272, respectively, while Loutraki, which we will visit in the next chapter, had 1,158 bathers and 12,192 baths taken, the highest recorded number in the section listing all the Loutropolis. The spring is recorded in the database as belonging to the municipality, and not to EOT. The report is damning of the state of the baths:"Destitute state, without shutters, closets, or sinks. Five of the natural baths are covered in dirt, plumbing in bad shape, cooling tank of low capacity, dire bathrooms, medical office installed in an unsuitable room." The permanent staff, however, indicates the desire from the municipality and the public for the baths to be operational, despite their poor condition. The same report indicates that the third-class facilities were at risk from the sea waves, while there was also a scarcity of food and ice. The outer walls lacked plaster. The terracotta roof tiles were in bad shape, and failed to keep the interiors dry. The report also comments on the question of ownership of the spring and the bath buildings as well as their future. Andreas Iatridis, *The Healing Springs of Greece* (Athens: EOT Report, 1951), table 5 (private archive). "The spring is of local importance; if there was a reason and large sums were spent to repair the damaged buildings, it would be possible [for it] to reach the second category easily, but neither the 'movement' nor the financial capacity of its customers allow this. . . . If the issue of its ownership is clarified in time, the service [EOT] can certainly propose fundamental improvements."
[22] The seminar week was organized in the framework of the Chair for the History of Art and Architecture, Philip Ursprung at gta Institute, ETH Zurich.
[23] Nikolaos Lekkas, *The 750 Mineral Springs of Greece* (Athens: A. Dialismas, 1938).
[24] Guided by the description found in Strabo's, Geographica the founder of these baths Dr. Pantelides published his findings, the curative properties of the springs and its ties to the Hippocratic curing tradition, in Pantélidis. "Peri ton archaion theiouchon thermon en Nisyro tou archipelagous (en grec)," *Bulletin de correspondance hellénique* 15, no. 1 (1891): 488–90, https://doi.org/10.3406/bch.1891.3839.
[25] Yet Nisyrian ground was to be claimed by many not only as a geopolitical territory, but also as a material. The soil, rich in sulfur, sparked interest from Greece, the Ottoman Empire, and Europe. Used to manufacture weapons, it later became an industrial enterprise. As Jeancard records: "The English colonizers, always zealous, had planted their flag there, in the hope of establishing a coal depot on the island. Projects quickly swallowed [it] up! And we agree that this close and unfortunate example is not made to encourage long-term speculation in Nisyros" (Flegel, *Asia Minor Baths*, 26).
[26] Primo Levi, *The Periodic Table*, trans. Raymond Rosenthal (New York: Schocken Books, 1984), 224.
[27] Calcium, sodium, potassium, and magnesium.
[28] Georgios Labrinopoulos, *Τα Λουτρά* [The Baths] (Athens: Sillogos pros Diadosin Ofelimon Vivliwn No. 95, 1908), 44.
[29] While bathing in sulfurous waters elsewhere, the current director of the Greek healing waters society told me that one does not need to be ill to take sulfur or the waters in general. The body absorbs and builds the minerals, preventing future illness.
[30] I sympathize with Aristotle: he felt uncomfortable with his contemporaries' explanation of nature. The atomists broke everything down to atoms, and the Platonists offered mathematical exhalations. His views offered a kind of nature that could be described through sensing.
[31] Ludwig Ross Otto, an archaeologist, who visited Nisyros on August 9–11, 1841. Quoted in *Niryriaka Chronika* (June 1955), 11.
[32] Flegel, *Asia Minor Baths*, 35.
[33] See also Lydia Xynogala, "The Vanishing Half Island: A (Not so) Ancient Myth," *Thresholds*, no. 52 (April 17, 2024): 146–55, https://doi.org/10.1162/thld_a_00823.
[34] GTP Headlines, "PM: New Tourism Investments to Position Greece in Ultra-Luxury Market," October 25, 2023, https://news.gtp.gr/2023/10/25/pm-new-tourism-investments-to-position-greece-in-ultra-luxury-market/.
[35] "I consider the first concern of the committee to be the study and preparation of a bill to be submitted to the Parliament and legalized, according to which the thermal waters should be declared as public assets because,due to their therapeutic purpose, they should not be objects of private use, nor municipal, since their operation does not aim at the enrichment of private persons nor the payment of the local needs of the municipalities, but the health of the community."

Anastasios Dambergis, “Peri tis skopimoteras dieuthetiseos twn en Elladi iamatikwn pigwn” [On the purposeful arrangement of the thermal springs in Greece] (Athens: Ethniko Typografeio, 1919).

[36] Elizabeth A. Povinelli, *Geontologies: A Requiem to Late Liberalism* (Durham: Duke University Press, 2016), 43.

[37] Anna L. Tsing, *The Mushroom at the End of the World: On the Possibility of Life in Capitalist Ruins* (Princeton: Princeton University Press, 2017), viii.

[38] At the time of completing the final draft for publication on December 2024 I have found out that a part of the abandoned “middle” bath building has just been demolished for the “renovation effort” adding another layer of urgency to this discussion on preservation of Loutra.

Figure 1. Installation view of the exhibition *The Architecture of the Ecole des Beaux-Arts*. October 29, 1975–January 4, 1976, MoMA. Photograph by David Allison. Source: The Museum of Modern Art Archives, New York. IN1110.1.

Barry Bergdoll and
Léa-Catherine Szacka

Conserving the Uncollectable?

Museum Exhibitions and Preservation Advocacy, 1942–1980

Introduction

In 1975 New York's Museum of Modern Art (MoMA) staged the instantly infamous exhibition *The Architecture of the Ecole des Beaux-Arts.* Generally associated with long-serving curator Arthur Drexler's seeming retreat from the museum's four decades of advocacy for modernism, the exhibition's multilayered agenda included, high on its priority list, a critique of urban renewal, via a celebration of the so-called Beaux-Arts city. But equally prominent—if rarely acknowledged today—was advocacy for historical preservation, in the wake of the loss of New York's Pennsylvania Station a decade earlier. In this, the controversial exhibition often analyzed for its relation to the rise of post-modernism,[1] also took part in a post–World War II engagement by museums in North America and in Europe in the rising movement for the conservation of nineteenth- and twentieth-century architecture, not simply through collecting architectural materials to be displayed in the museum, but for protecting buildings in situ in the public realm. This movement had already allied museums and grassroots advocates on a handful of occasions since the early twentieth century. But from the 1950s onward, powerful exhibiting institutions with a hold on public opinion and taste making staged events that garnered significant public and press attention.

From the late nineteenth century, with the founding of Skansen in Stockholm (1891), open-air museums saved buildings by moving them to *plein-air* settings, and soon thereafter the fashion for the installation of period rooms that preserved parts, even as whole buildings were removed from their historic contexts, gained currency from the Musée Carnavalet in Paris to countless US museums. But a new chapter in museums' engagement with historic preservation advocacy opened after World War II with the mounting of exhibitions of architectural heritage aimed to protect architecture that could not be relocated to a museum, and to reinforce the work of national and municipal organizations charged with designating heritage of relatively recent vintage. Advocacy for *in situ* preservation increasingly extended to city districts and fostered an understanding of urban morphology and a growing appreciation of the presence of history in cities. In the United States municipal preservation efforts were catalyzed by monumental losses to urban renewal, while in Britain vast social and political

Future Anterior
Volume XX, Numbers 1–2
Summer / Winter 2023

changes in cities and countryside resulted in the challenge of so-called redundant buildings, building types that were suddenly in surplus, notably churches. The institution of landmark plaques on buildings hoped to draw attention to the city as a living architecture museum, and museums joined in this new effort at historical memory, attempting to save buildings or districts in cities through provocative displays. From New York, beginning with MoMA's 1958 polemical *Architecture Worth Saving,* to London, with the Victoria and Albert Museum's dramatically staged *The Destruction of the Country House* (1974) and *The Future of Our Churches* (1977) to the Venice Biennale, with the confrontational 1975 *A Proposito del Molino Stucky*, internationally influential art institutions joined forces with local architectural preservation efforts.[2]

In recent years, much has been written about the history of the preservation movement in both the United States and the United Kingdom;[3] and a veritable industry has arisen in studying the history of architecture exhibitions, part of the institutional turn in architectural history.[4] Yet very little has been written on the intersection of these two histories. How can an exhibition make a case for preservation? What did it mean to try to have a building saved, not merely by protesting a proposed demolition in situ or by political engagement through the media, but, instead, or in addition, by turning to the already paradoxical and nearly impossible practice of bringing architecture—through representations—into the space of the gallery or the museum? What were the underlying politics of such exhibitions and to what extent might cultural institutions have been engaged in urban gentrification and the complexly intertwined class and racial stakes of preservation? How can we read the close temporal correspondence between the rise of architecture exhibitions and the parallel institutionalization of preservation? This short survey can only begin to offer case studies toward these questions, and cannot extend to cover other venues which a more comprehensive survey would include, such as the preservation agenda of the Centre Canadien d'Architecture, founded in 1979 by architect/preservationist Phyllis Lambert.[5]

Mainly chronological in scope, this article aims to highlight the key role of three major institutions cited above: New York's Museum of Modern Art (MoMA), London's Victoria & Albert (V&A) and the Venice Biennale. Starting with a preamble, this article identifies several exhibitions prior to this institutional engagement which were instrumental in earlier decades in shifting local attitudes about architectural preservation even as their international reach drew wider attention to the plight of nineteenth- and twentieth-century architecture in the ongoing waves of urban transformation.

Preamble: Museums and Local Heritage

Although the work of preservation organizations was often displayed in the context of the World's Fairs from the second half of the nineteenth century,[6] the earliest example of an exhibition in an art museum intended to raise public awareness was the 1942 exhibition *This Is Charleston*. From the 1920s Charleston, along with New Orleans, had been a pioneer in campaigns to save *in situ* historic buildings. Both cities were already famous tourist attractions for their architectural charms. But the preservation movements were set against two intertwined pressures: the real estate market and the growing antiques market in building parts. In 1924, as the Metropolitan Museum of Art opened its new American Wing with one of the largest sequences of period rooms yet assembled, the city of Charleston passed an ordinance creating "Old and Historic Charleston District," one of the oldest preservation laws in the United States, aimed at stemming the departure of building parts from the city's historic center to art museums. Efforts in Charleston played out against a rising market in salvaged parts, which became so brisk that it prompted the American Institute of Architects (AIA), in the early years of the Depression, to go on record urging museums not to incorporate historic interiors in their displays, except in the case of buildings legitimately on the brink of demolition.[7] In 1933 Franklin D. Roosevelt's Secretary of the Interior, Harold Ickes, was instrumental in establishing the Historic American Buildings Survey (HABS), which was tasked with creating measured drawings of historic structures throughout the country, a fundamental source of knowledge if not always a guarantee of protection.

During World War II, several important municipal architectural surveys were launched. These comprehensive efforts, which many historians see as a catalyst for an awakening of a patriotic concern with heritage, were at times linked with a public exhibition, the two meant to be tools toward the goal of preserving architectural heritage *in situ*. In 1942 the Carolina Art Association mounted *This Is Charleston* at the city's Gibbes Art Gallery to publicize the work of a 1940–41 survey, "one of the first . . . undertaken in a major American city and one of the earliest architectural inventories to be used as an urban planning tool."[8] In addition the growing popularity from the 1940s of architectural walking tours was also an integral part of the growing culture of preservation. As Robert Weyeneth notes in *Historic Preservation for a Living City* (2000), the exhibition consisted of thirty-four panels that offered an analysis of the city and its problems, stressing issues of housing, traffic, public health, recreation, and the physical appearance of the urban environment, along with information on the groups that had advocated for preserving Charleston's heritage. It ended with

Figure 2. *This is Charleston* exhibition press coverage (*left*) and invitation to the opening (*right*), 1942.

a wall mirror that made visitors exiting the exhibition the very last thing on show.[9] Above it was posted the question "Who is responsible for Charleston's future?" Intended to be traveled around the state, the local newspaper even asked if the exhibition should not be permanent.[10]

That an exhibition could be a technique for creating a public for preservation was immediately clear as attested to by press reactions. *The News and Courier* of Charleston noted: "Here is food for thought, here are answers to the questions of newcomers, here are unpleasant facts that will often offend civic pride and pleasant ones that make the chest swell. Here is a heritage and here is a challenge." The journalist continued enthusiastically, mentioning that there was no admission fee to encourage greatest possible attendance, but suggested that a visit "would not be free of mental effort," and yet "anyone who claims to think should not miss this opportunity."[11] The project had been put together by Helen Gardner McCormick, who had returned to her native Charleston after an innovative career at the Valentine museum of Richmond, Virginia, in 1941 to undertake a survey of Charleston architectural heritage.[12] The exhibition was followed by a guidebook, published in 1944, and to the institution of house tours, which became a standing feature of Charleston culture for years to come.[13] The show lived on in memory as well, recalled at the Gibbes some seventy-five years later with the show "Vanishing Charleston" on display from May to October 2018, a kind of booster shot needed in a city with escalating real estate prices and more and more second home owners.

No less was the history of preservation advocacy in New York City advanced through exhibitions as public awareness mechanisms. Here the Society of Architectural Historians (SAH), founded in 1940, was an important catalyst. In 1952 the Society planned to hold its twelfth annual meeting in New York. As preservation historian Anthony Wood has written "There is no doubt that the architectural historians" [. . .] conference provided the impetus that jump started serious work on the critically important inventory of significant New York buildings."[14] The key actor here was James Grote Van Derpool, SAH president and later the first executive director of the New York City Landmarks Preservation Commission, founded a decade later (1962). The survey was the joint effort of New York's Municipal Arts Society (MAS) and the SAH. And soon plans were afoot for an exhibition to be on view during the national convention which would bring architectural historians from around the country to New York in January 1952. *Thirty New York Buildings Most Worthy of Preservation,* staged at the Museum of the City of New York, was composed largely of didactic illustrated panels. As at Charleston there was a participatory element: this time a ballot box for visitors to vote on which building they considered most worthy of protection. St. Mark's Church in-the-Bowery (c. 1795) emerged as the most popular candidate although, interestingly, buildings of the early twentieth century, such as the Woolworth Building (1910–13), were also included in the display and received votes. A pendant exhibition of buildings "of historical and architectural note which are now fully protected" was mounted in the Pine Room of the Architectural League, then still in the building it shared with the Art Students League on West 57th Street.

Threats were coming more and more frequently. By 1953, there was serious talk in New York of demolishing Grand Central Terminal to make way for an office tower; while in 1954 real estate developer William Zeckendorf, who had optioned the air rights of McKim, Mead & White's Pennsylvania Station, hinted that demolition of that historic Beaux-Arts train station might also be in the cards. Nor were these historic rail termini alone in the cross hairs of development. By that spring the Committee to Save Carnegie Hall had been formed. The 1952 exhibition soon generated others, including *Monuments of Manhattan: Great Buildings in New York City, 1800–1918*, curated by Henry Hope Reed and staged at McKim, Mead & White's University Club, one of the buildings on the list. It was on view from January 1 to March 15, 1955.[15] Color coding was used on the exhibition labels: buildings considered of national significance were pointed out in red, white, and blue; buildings of local importance in the colors of the city flag; while buildings that had been lost were draped in black and those threatened highlighted in red. Unlike earlier exclusively photographic exhibitions, this display included models, tracings, photographs, original drawings, and renderings, and billed itself as an early venture into the preservation of architectural records and drawings. Hope had sought out documents even among architects' descendants and reproduced some in the brochure.[16]

While access to the display was by invitation only in this bastion of white upper-class male privilege—reminding us of the extent to which preservation was very often exclusionary of other voices—it served as the clearing house for newspaper articles, radio programs and served thus to broadcast the message "that we would be foolish to let our heritage be carried away by the tide of modern fashion."[17] One thousand copies of the MAS's *Buildings in Manhattan Built Before World War I Worthy of Protection* were distributed. Reed began the walking tours for which he was soon to be famous, and which have remained a mainstay of the activities of the Municipal Art Society to this day. In 1955 the program of Landmark Plaques was launched.

By 1957 the scene had moved to Brooklyn where the Long Island Historical Society in Brooklyn Heights mounted the display *Classical Brooklyn: Its Architecture and Sculpture*. One of the outcomes, a few years later, in 1965, was the designation of Brooklyn Heights as the first historic district under New York's new Landmarks Law.

New York's Museum of Modern Art as Advocate for Preservation

Advocacy had been the ethos of the Museum of Modern Art's architecture exhibitions from the foundation of the Department of Architecture in 1932 with displays intended as agents for change as much as historical retrospectives. Famously, the inaugural exhibition *Modern Architecture: International Exhibition*, in 1932, had coined the term "International Style,"

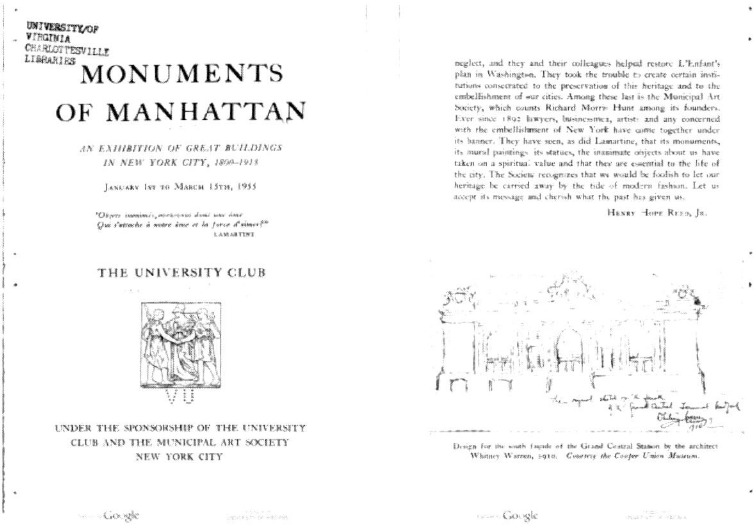

Figure 3. *Monuments of Manhattan: An Exhibition of Great Buildings in New York City, 1800–1918* exhibition brochure, cover (*left*) and final page with illustration of Whitney Warren's drawing of the south facade of Grand Central Terminal (*right*). The University Club, New York, 1955. Source: University of Virginia Library.

advocating for a stylistic paradigm shift in American architectural design, one in which United States practice might catch up with European avant-gardes. It had been followed by exhibitions advocating for housing reform, as well as displays mounted rapidly to protest initiatives from the probable conservatism of an announced model village, *The Town of Tomorrow*, planned for the New York World's Fair in 1939 to advocacy for a modernist approach to the future United Nations Headquarters once the New York site was announced for the new international organization. In 1958, the Museum would join the rising cause of conservation, extending its influence advocating for preservation and not simply for new architecture. Here the museum responded, perhaps in part, to a position pioneered by Lucio Costa in Brazil in the 1930s and highlighted in MoMA's 1942 *Brazil Builds*—that modernism and preservation were allies rather than adversaries.

The context was Urban Renewal, the clearing of entire city districts in the 1950s, given its most advanced form perhaps in the old commercial cores of St. Louis, cleared to create a park-like setting for Saarinen's Jefferson Expansion Arch, and of Philadelphia with a new *mise-en-scène* of Independence Hall. The irony was that to create a frame of empty space around Independence Hall, and other monuments associated with patriotic history, a whole district of vintage architecture from the nineteenth and early twentieth centuries was to be cleared after the Pennsylvania state legislature authorized the creation of Independence State Park in October 1945. Some 143 buildings in the area—among them very significant buildings designed by such noted Philadelphia architects as Addison Hutton and Frank Furness, along with the proto-skyscraper Jayne Building (1870) by John McArthur Jr. and the city's first

Figure 4. Philadelphia's Independence Hall before clearance in 1950, looking north from Walnut Street, in the area that would become Independence Mall. Source: The Philadelphia Inquirer Archive.

Figure 5. Philadelphia's Independence Hall in 1952, after the demolition of a building to make way for Independence Mall. Photo courtesy of PhillyHistory .org, a project of the Philadelphia Department of Records.

true steel frame building, the Drexel Building—were demolished, beginning in 1952. Only structures built prior to 1800 were to remain in the historic district. And this, despite the protests of National Park Service Architect Charles Peterson, who recorded his views, and his findings on the buildings about to be lost, in the *Journal of the Society of Architectural Historians*. With the SAH planning its January 1954 meeting in Philadelphia these planned demolitions became a delicate issue and the protests, largely in the press and letter writing, continued for several years.[18] Philip Johnson at the Museum of Modern Art was one of many to write to Judge Edwin O. Lewis—who had set in motion a decade earlier the move to reclaim the Independence Hall area—in protest of the loss of what he said were "some of the finest buildings in Philadelphia." "I most regret the Furness Bank in front of Carpenter's Hall, but much more than my personal feeling is the loss to Philadelphia of a building by its greatest architect. Furness was a giant among pigmies," Johnson wrote. "If we in the United States are to join in the cultural life of the Western World, we cannot allow the whims of commerce to dictate what buildings will be preserved for our common heritage and what will be destroyed."[19] With the influence of New York's museum at his command, Johnson threatened to organize a protest exhibition at MoMA with the proposed title *Philadelphia Tears Down Its Monuments,* a threat never fulfilled. The judge was quick to respond: "These buildings are out of character with the older buildings to be preserved in Independence National Historical Park and do not belong to the Colonial or Federal period of Philadelphia's history. These buildings are interesting only to architects and it seems to us that photographs will suffice to preserve their appearance and dimensions."[20] Yale architectural historian Carroll L. V. Meeks, past president of the SAH and member of the AIA Committee on the Preservation of Historic Buildings also wrote urging the retention of these witnesses to the "vigor and creative originality of the American of the 19th century."[21] Lewis Mumford weighed in the pages of the *New Yorker,* with a four-part article in which he developed a veritable portrait of the positions in the nascent preservation movement between those who sought unity of style in a chosen moment of the past—the time of the signing of the Declaration of Independence in this case—and those who saw the city as a living palimpsest. Mumford advocated even for allowing contemporary design a place in redevelopment of the areas now being treated as a historical park by the National Park Service, to the east of Independence Hall as well as the three-block esplanade that the state of Pennsylvania was creating to form a monumental axial frame for Independence Hall closer to the spirit of L'Enfant's Washington, DC, than to colonial Philadelphia. He condemned the pseudo-eighteenth-century buildings being added to the district, noting with characteristic biting satire that "So far, the reconstruction of the district has been treated principally as a problem of insulation—and effort to keep the Twentieth Century from intruding on the Eighteenth, or at least persuading it to put on a hired fancy-dress costume, dated Eighteenth century but fabricated of nylon and held together by zippers whenever it comes near the older quarters." Mumford used the large-scale operation underway in Philadelphia to advocate for an urban renewal that could include historic preservation. This reflected a position he had already pronounced years earlier, in 1938, in his widely read *The Culture of Cities*: "I stand firmly with the present administrators of the Park Service and against the "total preservationists." [. . .] I would like to quote from *The Culture of Cities*: "If the city is to escape being a confused rubbish heap, the function of preservation and storage must be taken over by the museum. . . . By confining the role of preservation to the museum, we thus release space in the rest of the city for the fresh uses of the city."[22]

If the threatened show on Philadelphia's destruction of heritage never took place, MoMA soon took a strong stance in the emerging debates over historic preservation and urban renewal, opening the exhibition *Architecture Worth Saving* on October 8, 1958. The show was co-sponsored by the nine-year-old National Trust for Historic Preservation and by *Architectural Forum* magazine. "The preservation of America's 18th-century architecture now enjoys public sympathy and support," wrote Arthur Drexler, Johnson's successor as Director of the Department of Architecture and Design, in the press release, "but many great buildings of the 19th and early 20th centuries—too recent to seem romantic or significant—have not yet aroused public interest and are being ruthlessly destroyed. The Museum of Modern Art, which has always championed the cause of a creative modern architecture, is concerned with this problem because unless the habit of preservation prevails there can be no architecture at all, and today's great buildings will soon disappear in their turn."[23]

In its founding years MoMA conceived itself as radically of the present, with Alfred Barr's famous diagram of the torpedo speeding through history, leaving a trail of deaccession of anything over several decades old to become part of the permanent collections of the Metropolitan or Whitney Museums. But from the outset the Department of Architecture (later of Architecture and Design) imagined both a projective and retrospective role for its exhibitions, laid out in a multiyear plan drawn up by architectural historian Henry-Russell Hitchcock. Hitchcock imagine an episodic series of exhibitions that would do the same thing he was doing in his writings, namely tracing the contours and establishing a canon of significant buildings that would constitute the history of modernism since the eighteenth century.[24] Some of the buildings featured in large photographs had been exhibited before at MoMA in Hitchcock's displays, notably those by Richardson, Sullivan, and Wright, whom the Museum had helped cast as America's founding fathers of modernist architecture. Not only had Wright—whose Guggenheim was then under construction even as MoMA lamented the replacement of Wright's Larkin Building in the press release—been the subject of more exhibitions at MoMA than any other architect; but the museum had devoted two exhibitions to Richardson, one in 1936 and another in 1947. For the later the texts were written by a young curatorial assistant: Ada Louise Huxtable, the future architecture critic of the *New York Times*. Huxtable and Hitchcock also worked together in 1948 on a Louis Sullivan exhibition.

Figure 6. Installation view of the exhibition *Architecture Worth Saving*, October 8–December 15, 1958, MoMA. Photograph by Soichi Sunami. Source: The Museum of Modern Art Archives, New York (images of H. H. Richardson).

In 1958 threats to works by these great proto modernists was very much the theme: "H.H. Richardson's masterpiece the Allegheny County Jail in Pittsburgh, completed in 1886 after the death of the pioneer architect, is slated for demolition unless a new use such as a museum can found for the 'noble interior and stone walled courts,'" the museum noted to sound an alarm. No less alarming was the situation with Sullivan and Adler's Auditorium building in Chicago, which "stands empty and crumbling because its owners, Roosevelt University, cannot obtain funds to repair it despite its basic soundness, good location, and excellent acoustics."[25] In its June 1958 issue, *Architectural Forum*—which provided a catalogue in the form of an offprint from the magazine—underscored that the lead in destruction was being taken by the US Congress itself with its plan "to extend the east front of the Capital," which "would trade an improvement of doubtful value and fabulous cost for the few existent stones of the original Capitol." Among the losses was Belle Grove, one of the most famed plantation houses in Louisiana, along with cast iron buildings in St. Louis, Missouri, that had been cleared to make way for architect Eero Saarinen's Jefferson National Expansion Memorial. Even the Brooklyn Bridge and Greenwich Village's Washington Square—on which Robert Moses had set his sights—were not in the clear, or rather might be cleared. *Forum* gave a very cogent analysis of the complex factors endangering buildings.

Beyond the march of so-called progress insensitive remodeling was a great a threat: "most architects think they can "improve" anything."[26] "Architecture Worth Saving" was sent on a nationwide tour, beginning at the Octagon Gallery, the headquarters of the American Institute of Architects, in Washington, DC, in March 1959. But the most immediate success of the touring exhibition were iterations that took up the initiative of MoMA to showcase historic architecture and to make the case for saving local architecture heritage.[27]

Ada Louise Huxtable, now the first ever architecture critic of *The New York Times* gave the show full coverage, explaining that the alliance of the Museum and the National Trust for Historic Preservation was not as strange as it might appear in facing the "current cultural crisis: the destruction of our architectural heritage."[28] "In defending this architecture and asking for its protection, the museum is, as usual, ahead of its time. Slow-moving public taste will probably require another generation to appreciate the value of what is being destroyed today. Many of these buildings are not only outstanding contributions to the art of architecture, but their unique design and engineering advances are the foundation of the contemporary style that the museum has so effectively championed for so long." Huxtable also pointed out what she saw as a "curious anachronism," since at the same time as nineteenth and early twentieth century buildings were being destroyed or left to decay, "we are enthusiastically reconstructing eighteenth century buildings that suffered a similar fate at an earlier time." Huxtable also cites the reconstruction of Williamsburg, a project backed, like MoMA, by the Rockefellers: "This false-false architecture, with its romantic game of make-believe, is usurping the major part of our energies and enthusiasm while we close our eyes to the tragic loses close at hand."[29]

In 1966 the campaign for preservation extended for the first time to a building the museum had already shown as contemporary architecture but three decades earlier when Drexler mounted a quick response to news of threats to one of the masterworks of the recently deceased Le Corbusier. *Villa Savoye: Destruction through Neglect* shown for a few weeks in July 1966 was intended to shame the French government into saving the famous villa from decay and degradation.[30] The model of the building in MoMA's collection had itself been restored, and refreshed for the display, set against images of a decaying original.

In subsequent MoMA shows preservation was often more an implicit message, notably in the 1967 exhibition *The New City*, which sought alternatives to large scale clearance for urban renewal. No less was preservation at stake in the more oblique critique of urban renewal postulated by

Figure 7. Installation view of *Villa Savoye: Destruction through Neglect*, July 2–24, 1966, MoMA. Photograph by George Cserna. Source: The Museum of Modern Art Archives, New York.

The Architecture of the Ecole des Beaux-Arts show in 1975. In unexpected ways,[31] the "Beaux-Arts show"—a shocking admission of the academy into the temple of the avant-garde—was intended as a sweeping critique of the modernist city. In the wake of two decades of American urban redevelopment, which had led to so much massive destruction of the legacy of the nineteenth century and of American Beaux-Arts monuments, notably the demolition of New York's Pennsylvania Station in 1963 and the repeated threats to Grand Central Terminal, the museum would now add its galleries to the site where protests were staged. "It is scarcely surprising," Drexler noted in April 1974, "that once again architects agree about very little concerning the nature of their art. Indeed, if there is one thing about which they do agree, at least enough to sign manifestos and march on picket lines, it is the necessity of preserving what is left of Beaux-Arts architecture, wherever it might be found."[32]

Critics immediately understood. Writing in the *Boston Globe,* Robert Campbell declared that "Only a fool would believe that the exhibition is really about the Architecture of the Ecole des Beaux-Arts."[33] The *Wall Street Journal* asked, "Is this supposed to reflect a major shift in contemporary architecture or is this merely revivalism? After all," they continued with reference to a recent show on nineteenth-century French

Figure 8. American writer Jane Jacobs (*left*) and architect Philip Johnson (*right*) stand with picketing crowds outside Penn Station to protest the building's demolition, New York City. Placards read: "AGBANY is here" and "Save Penn Station." Photograph by Walter Daran. Source: Hulton Archive/Getty Images.

Figure 9. Installation view of *The Architecture of the Ecole des Beaux-Arts*, October 29, 1975–January 4, 1976, MoMA. Photograph by David Allison. Source: The Museum of Modern Art Archives, New York.

academic art at the Metropolitan Museum, "technology and futuristic ideas aren't very popular at the moment but delving into the 19th century certainly is."[34] It was Huxtable who, as so often, had the most pertinent take. Under the title "Beaux-Arts: The Latest Avant Garde," she captured the essence of the gesture:

Figure 10. Installation view of *The Architecture of the Ecole des Beaux-Arts*, October 29, 1975–January 4, 1976, MoMA (view with photographs of American buildings). Photograph by David Allison. Source: The Museum of Modern Art Archives, New York.

> The exhibition is obviously about to break a taboo. It is going to make the architectural Academy respectable again, as is already happening with the Academy in painting and sculpture. At its deepest level, it urges us to examine the 'moral imperative' of utility and sociology, the modernist doctrine that is the basis of today's building. That is attacking a very sacred cow. But the show has brought a lot of beautiful drawings and hidden history out of the closet. . . . The Museum of Modern Art is still performing its charter job of questioning the established order. This time, it is the order that it helped establish. And if it is making waves by looking backward, that is the nature of our times.[35]

With the drama of spotlighting and the introduction of a processional axis in the spirt of Beaux-Arts ceremonial planning, Drexler staged the largest show of architectural drawings to date at MoMA, breaking with the Architecture Department's long tradition of featuring documentary photographic displays punctuated by a few select models. Drexler was keen to underscore that he was not endorsing any literal revival of the monumental classicism of the Beaux-Arts tradition, something which would gain more and more adherents in the coming years particularly as the show was adopted by John Barrington Bayley and his friends at "Classical America."[36] Rather, he was eager to use the French Beaux-Arts to leverage a debate over modernism's lack of interest in context and historical precedent, and in particular its place in the period's large scale urban redevelopment—something that Jane Jacobs had already criticized in her influential and popular *Death and Life of Great American Cities* of 1961—and of the growing cleavage between social purpose and architectural education, particularly in the large scale adoption of the architectural model as an end to itself. If his ideas were only partially formed in 1975, by the time of the belated publication of the catalogue in 1977, on the other side of a storm of debate and controversy sparked by the event, his ideas were firm.

As he was planning the show, Drexler had wavered between using the Beaux-Arts to suggest that the Modern Movement itself had become a new academy, rigid and unquestioned, and suggesting that one might, as Robert Venturi would soon put it, learn "the right lessons" from the Beaux-Arts.[37] Drexler had sold the idea to his fellow curators at a meeting in January 1974 with the argument that "What the Beaux Arts and modern movement had in common were the convictions that architecture can be taught; that good teaching leads to good practice; that architects must sit in judgment on the societies for which they build; and that architects must be given the opportunity to build at ever larger scale, even if this requires modification of the social order." While Drexler praised the modern movement's ability to create singular masterpieces, many of which had been shown repeatedly in exhibitions at the museum over the decades, he admitted that these had "not cancelled out its disastrous failures in urban planning," adding that "it is in urban planning that Beaux-Arts principles were most effective, not only in sustaining the character of the urban environment but in handling individual buildings at any scale. A Beaux-Arts architect was not so much interested in urbanism as being urbane."[38]

The preservation of urban values, as much as the preservation of individual monuments, were celebrated in the gallery of black and white photographs of American Beaux-Arts buildings that rounded out the show. From the World's Columbian Exposition to the urban situation of Grand Central Terminal the photographs argued for the preservation of civic values that were falling to the urban renewal bulldozers along with the Beaux-Arts classical detailing.

V&A: The Peril of Redundant Nineteenth-Century Heritage

In England, the case of the 1974 exhibition *The Destruction of the Country House, 1875–1975*, presented at the Victoria & Albert Museum is recognized as a milestone in the battle for preservation.[39] As Ruth Adams noted, "the exhibition played a key role in shaping the discourse and advancing the public awareness and political efficacy of the heritage movement [. . .]

Figure 11. Poster of the exhibition *The Destruction of the Country House, 1875–1975*, Victoria and Albert Museum, London, 1974. Source: V&A Archives.

from a minority interest to a cause with significant popular appeal and support."[40] On view from September to December, the display was commissioned by the museum's director Roy Strong and assembled by architectural historian John Harris, curator of the Royal Institute of British Architect's drawing collection and director of its architectural gallery together with both Marcus Binney, editor of *Country Life* magazine, and Peter Thornton, keeper in the V&A's Department of furniture and woodwork. The main message that country houses could represent a form of "heritage" that needed to be rescued added a whole new focus to the British preservation movement's priorities, focused attention on church architecture and on the countryside respectively, and on much earlier phases of architectural history.[41]

The exhibition had been conceived following a conversation between Strong, and architectural historian John Cornforth, then compiling an important report on the "present" state of Britian's country houses, the first since the Gowers Report, published in June 1950 following the creation, in 1948, of a UK Government committee to look at "Houses of Outstanding Historic or Architectural Interest." The Gowers report, which marked a seminal moment in the postwar rescue of Britain's country house heritage, led to the establishment of the Historic Building Council with the power to make annual grants for the restoration of significant buildings, the creation of the Grade listing system for preservation in the UK, and to tax concessions to which owners would be entitled, and financial assistance for which they may be eligible. The aim was to create a legal framework where restrictions on the rights of private owners were compensated by financial incentives to ensure the preservation of their houses.

The show aimed to highlight how, since 1875, an alarming number of country homes across the British Isles had been demolished due to falling estate incomes, rising costs, and death duties, compounding the damage caused by government requisitioning during World War II. The phenomenon was called by some a "cultural tragedy" as the loses reached dramatic proportions (In 1955 for instance, it is said that a country house was demolished every five days). Conceived as a multimedia affair, the display included paintings, photographs, furniture, furnishing and audio-visual elements, all dramatically staged. Most memorable was the "Hall of Lost Houses," also sometimes called the Hall of Destruction, a fantasy of tumbling columns with, on each piece of "falling" masonry a photograph of one of the thousand or so country houses demolished over the preceding century. The environment, designed by innovative Australian-born museum designer Robin Wade (who would later be known for his spectacular, yet controversial Egyptian

Figure 12. "Hall of Lost Houses," part of the exhibition *The Destruction of the Country House, 1875–1975* Victoria & Albert Museum, London, 1974. Source: V&A Archives.

sculpture galleries at the British Museum) also included a background audio tape playing "sounds of burning timbers and collapsing buildings with the voice of John Harris reading the names of lost country seats 'like a litany.'" According to Adams: "it was deliberately staged to wring an emotional reaction from visitors, perhaps reflecting the 'passion' with which it was produced."[42] The message of the exhibition also reached beyond the walls of the museum thanks to a best-selling book and a BBC2 television program (written and presented by Strong and produced by David Cheshire) called *Gone, Going, Going: The Fate of the Country House.*[43] The immense publicity and concern generated by *The Destruction of the Country House* put a virtual halt to demolition of country houses after 1975. The exhibition was also legendary in sparking the creation of SAVE Britain's Heritage, a group of architects, journalists and planners who came together in 1975 with the aim to provide a strong, independent voice in conservation, capable of responding quickly to emergencies.

After the success of *The Destruction of the Country House*, the V&A organized two further exhibitions on British architectural heritage: *Change and Decay: The Future of our Churches* (1977), curated by Strong with Marcus Binney and Peter Burman and *The Garden: A Celebration of a Thousand Years of British Gardening* (1979), organized by John Harris. While *The Destruction of the Country House*, began with a celebration and went on to the famous "Hall of Destruction," for *Change and Decay* exhibition designer Barry Mazur adopted the opposite strategy: he started with "a harrowing large format slide show of demolition followed by the glories of church art and positive examples of rescue and reuse,"[44] including theatre, museums, creches, youth clubs, workshops, etc. He then used dramatic means by combining a series of fragments—like carved ornamental details, stained-glass windows, churches sculptures, church furniture, fonts, lecterns, and masses of photos of fine

Figure 13. Cover, catalogue of the exhibition *Change and Decay: The Future of Our Churches*, Victoria & Albert Museum, London, 1977. Source: V&A Archives.

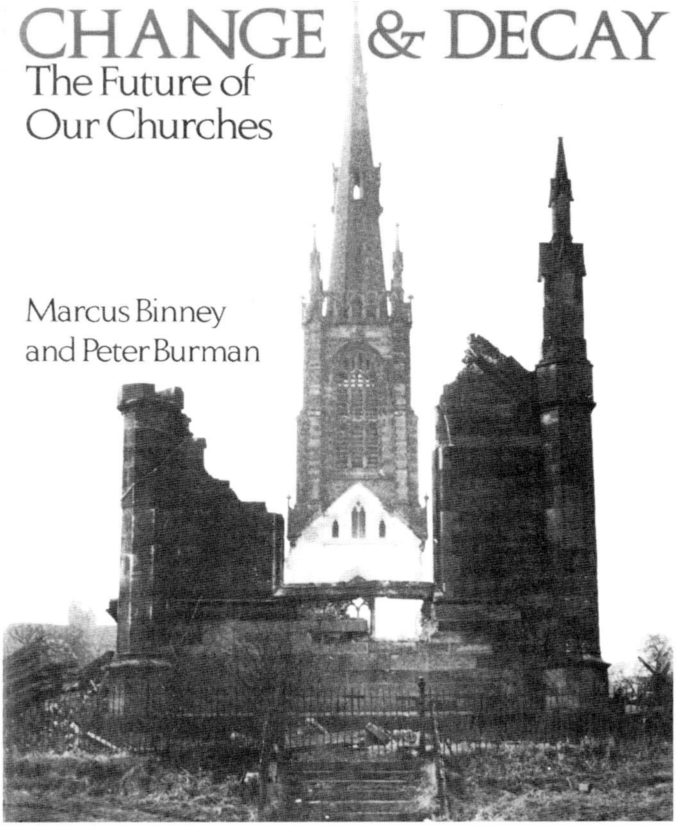

specimens at risk and already lost—placing them against a background of soft Handel music. The exhibition also included a "rash of incriminating facts" such as "in 1975 the church commissioners authorized the demolition of one church every nine days, and the Church of England is the only denomination which does not need to obtain consent to demolish a listed building."[45]

Although today not as well remembered as *The Destruction of the Country House*, the church exhibition was nonetheless highly influential: It was followed up by a large travelling version consisting of "eighty-six-foot-high panels which opened like books to reveal magnificent photographs of churches, lost, decayed and revived"[46] and toured the country for three years, shown at museums and galleries, and even cathedrals. Following the exhibition, government grants for church repair dramatically improved the outlook for historic churches in England. "There is a new alarm about the condition of the churches" said *Observer* journalist Patrick O'Donovan in a long piece published on 28 August 1977, in conjunction with the exhibition.[47]

Venice Biennale as *Agent Provocateur* for Creativity

During these same years, at the Venice Biennale, another internationally influential cultural institution, discourse on preservation and actual salvage of buildings intertwined, during what can be considered the institution's first attempts at putting architecture on display.[48] In 1975, the Biennale organized an international competition by invitation to prefigure the possibility of a creative reuse of the neo-gothic Molino Stucky, a by then disused flour mill built between 1884 and 1895 on the western end of the Giudecca Island by German architect Ernst Wullekopf. Rather than soliciting real projects, the competition sought to trigger a process that could draw general considerations on the relationship between collective creativity and the image of the city. Participation was not limited to architects, but open equally to visual artists. Joseph Beuys, Walter de Maria, Claes Oldenburg, and Jean Tinguely all sent proposals. The competition entries were exhibited and reproduced in an accompanying publication[49] and were judged by a jury that included, alongside "experts," residents of Venice. If some critics claimed that the exhibition *Proposals for the Stucky Mill*, presented as a concrete recovery operation of the old factory, turned out to be a sterile and evasive intellectualist operation incapable of producing real projects, it nevertheless raised the problem of preservation in such a way that the building could hardly be demolished or abandoned to real estate speculation. In this the Biennale as an institution acted as an *agent provocateur*, inciting something more serious than what might have first met the eye. Francesco Dorigo noted in the Vatican's newspaper *L'Osservatore Romano*: "If everything was limited to a game, albeit a pleasant one, by artists in the mood to joke, then the intended aim was not achieved. If, on the other hand, the Biennale with its proposal open to the imagination of the artists wanted to create an atmosphere of dissent and protest against a radical-Marxist art and culture, then it succeeded."[50]

What perhaps distinguishes the Venetian case from the British and United States examples is this highly speculative and artistic component. The exhibition did not raise awareness by impressive scenographic effects, but rather served as an incubator for new ideas directly engaging the public. A series of dialogues collected by the Environmedia group (a group created by the Biennale to trigger a serious exchange around urban intervention and collective creativity with the inhabitants of the Giudecca island) revealed that the workers of the island felt in need of a hospital, but also a kindergarten, a row of houses for the workers, a hospice, and even a university: but that no one wanted the Molino Stucky to be demolished.[51] Yet, according to Vittorio Gregotti, then chief curator of the art and architecture Biennale, the exhibition raised the problem in such a way that the Stucky mill would be unlikely to be demolished for reasons of building speculation.[52]

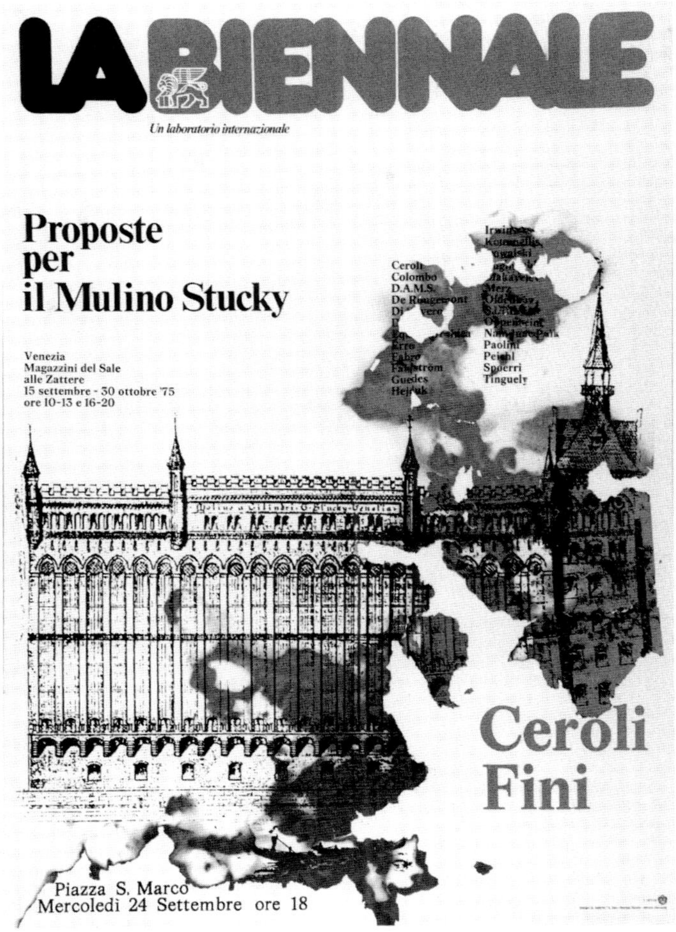

Figure 14. Poster of the exhibition *Proposte per il Mulino Stucky*, Biennale di Venezia, 1975. Source: The Historical Archives of Contemporary Arts (ASAC), La Biennale di Venezia.

Figure 15. Perspective view of John Hejduk's "Cemetery of the Ashes of Thought" for the exhibition *Proposals for the Stucky Mill*, 1975. Source: The Historical Archives of Contemporary Arts (ASAC), La Biennale di Venezia.

Proposals for the Stucky Mill came at a crucial time in the history of demolitions of nineteenth century industrial architecture. Just a few years earlier prior, between 1971 and 1973, the demolition of the iron and glass pavilions of Paris's central market (Les Halles) designed in 1852 by Victor Baltard had aroused widespread opposition, including a petition with

Figure 16. Magazzini del Sale, Zattere, Venice, 1975. Source: Photo Archive Lorenzo Capellini.

some one hundred thousand signatures.[53] Writing in *Le Monde*, journalist Sabine Marchand pointed out that "Usually, architects are called on in competitions for the revitalization of a neighborhood in a large city. And it is for this reason that the experiment proposed by the Biennale is worthy of attention. In fact, the French had dreamed of a broad consultation of this kind for Les Halles. Will Venice set an example?"[54] But despite this hopeful call from Paris, the Venice exhibition was criticized locally for its lack of concreteness.

From the late 1970s, exhibitions in Venice began to be held in disused monuments—churches, palaces, warehouses, and most famously the former navy arsenal (*Arsenale*). These exhibitions literally saved Venetian buildings by giving them a new life.[55] This way the 1975 exhibition was a precursor since it was first thought to mount the display in the abandoned mill.[56] This was thwarted when the Società Litoranea-Istituto Romano dei Beni Stabili, owners of the mill, refused access to the building, claiming that the Biennale's actions constituted a dangerous aesthetic bribe. Ultimately, the exhibition was presented at the Magazzini del Sale (Salt Warehouse) on the Zattere Canal, another building slated for imminent demolition. Monument to the economic power and the mercantile heritage of Venice, the Magazzini del Sale likewise became the object of a fierce preservation battle following the unanimous vote of the City Council on December 7, 1973, to demolish the building to make way for a swimming-pool, "hollowing out" the insides and leaving only the perimeter walls intact.

Figure 17. V&A exhibition *Robin Hood Gardens: A Ruin in Reverse*, part of the 16th Venice Architecture Biennale, 2018. Photo: Dezeen. Source: V&A Archives.

Conclusion

Looking at the history of the preservation through the lens of display this article demonstrates that architecture exhibitions have often served political engagement, advocating for the preservation of historic buildings, and thus becoming agents for change. By examining a series of exhibitions that advocated for the preservation of individual buildings and/or historic urban fabric in different *modus operandi*, we highlight the crucial role played by museums and other cultural institutions in the protection of nineteenth- and twentieth-century architecture in the US, the UK, and Italy. By aiming at conserving what they cannot collect, institutions such as the Museum of Modern Art, the Victoria and Albert Museum or the Venice Biennale set up a critical relationship between the museum and their respective cities. And, if in the Anglo-American context we first see the role of the institution as agent which contribute to raising interest and awareness for preservation and thus crafting a specific type of public, in the Italian context, the institution also helped by proposing solutions and fostering creativity through the blurring of boundaries between art and architecture, suggesting therefore a movement toward practices of adaptive reuse.

Salvaging fragments for museological display launched in the early nineteenth century has had a long afterlife. In 2018, the V&A moved a 9m-high salvaged section of the façade of London's Robin Hood Gardens (1972), a famed Brutalist housing estate designed by Alison and Peter Smithson that had been the object of a long and ultimately failed preservation attempt, to Venice, for the exhibition *Robin Hood Gardens: A Ruin in Reverse*, part of the 16th Venice Architecture Biennale. Organized in the midst of the polemic surrounding the demolition of the estate, the exhibition was also the occasion of displaying the salvaged section, recently acquired by the museum for its permanent collection. From May to October 2018, the Gibbes museum in Charleston renewed its appeal for preservation with the show *Vanishing Cha*rleston. If 1974–75 marked a critical threshold in the history of preservation of the modern, the paradoxical relationship between historic architecture in the city and political and cultural power of museum institutions continues today, marking their contemporary relevance as 'voice' within larger cultural debates. Indeed, from *Lost Vanguard* (2007) surveying the extent and often decayed condition of modernist architecture in the former Soviet Union to the recent exhibitions featuring the brutalist architecture of the former Yugoslavia (2019) and of South Asia (2022), MoMA's historical surveys and the call for preservation have become joined agendas. What we have proposed here is but a first contribution which might serve as an invitation to further study not only of the linked fates of museum exhibitions and architectural preservation, but also the task of preserving the memory of significant ephemeral displays in institutions and geographies beyond the purview of this essay.

Biographies

Barry Bergdoll is Meyer Schapiro Professor of Art History at Columbia University. He served from 2007 to 2014 as Chief Curator of Architecture & Design at the Museum of Modern Art (NY), where he curated numerous exhibitions and installations on modern architecture and on contemporary issues in architecture and landscape. He is the author of publications accompanying those exhibitions as well as a widely used textbook *European Architecture: 1750–1890* in the Oxford History of Art series (2000), monographs on Karl Friedrich Schinkel (1994) Mies van der Rohe (2001), Léon Vaudoyer (1994), and (as editor) *Marcel Breuer: Building Global Institutions* (2017). He is at work on a volume on the history of exhibiting architecture, derived from the Mellon Lectures at the National Gallery of Art in Washington in 2013 and an exhibition on the drawings of French architect Viollet-le-Duc for 2026.

Léa-Catherine Szacka is Senior Lecturer (Associate Professor) in Architectural Studies at the University of Manchester and director of the Manchester Architecture Research Group (MARG). Since 2024, she has been vice-president of the European Architectural History Network (EAHN). She was also visiting lecturer at Harvard Study Abroad Program (2018), the Berlage Center for Advanced Studies in Architecture and Urban Design (2019 to 2024), the ETH-Zurich (2020–21) and the EPFL Lausanne (2024). Szacka is the author of *Exhibiting the Postmodern: The 1980 Venice Architecture Biennale* (2016) and *Biennials/Triennials: Conversations on the Geography of Itinerant Display* (2019). She is also co-author of *Le Concert: Pink Floyd à Venise* (2017) and *Paolo Portoghesi: Architecture between History,Politics and Media* (2023), as well as coeditor of *Mediated Messages: Periodicals, Exhibitions and the Shaping of Postmodern Architecture* (2018) and *Concrete Oslo* (2018). In 2022, she co-curated the 10th International Architecture Biennale of Rotterdam, "It's About Time."

Notes

[1] See, for example, Felicity Scott, "When Systems Fail: Arthur Drexler and the Postmodern Turn," *Perspecta 35: Building Codes* (2004): 152–71; Alice Thomine, "Les Beaux-Arts au MOMA: Consécration du post-modernisme ou naissance de

l'histoire de l'architecture du xixe siècle?," in Gérard Monnier, ed., *L'architecture: La réception immédiate et la réception différée. L'œuvre jugée, l'édifice habité, le monument célébré* (Paris: Editions de la Sorbonne, 2006), 123–38; Barry Bergdoll, "Complexities and Contradictions of Post-Modern Classicism: Notes on the Museum of Modern Art's 1975 Exhibition, 'The Architecture of the Ecole des Beaux-Arts,'" *The Persistence of the Classical, Essays on Architecture Presented to David Watkin,* ed. Frank Salmon (London: Philip Wilson, 2008), 202–17; Jean-Philippe Garric, "L'architecture Beaux-Arts. Objet d'expositions," in *Les Cahiers du Musée d'art moderne,* no. 129 (automne 2014): 38–49; and Thomas S. Hines, *Architecture and Design at the Museum of Modern Art: The Arthur Drexler Years, 1951–1986* (Los Angeles: Getty Publications, 2019).

[2] A shorter version of this paper was presented at the 2021 SAH Annual International Conference in Montreal (online) on April 16, 2021 in the session organized by Elizabeth Keslacy. We are grateful to her and our fellow panelists in that stimulating session for comments and suggestions.

[3] See, for example, Randall F. Mason and Max Page, eds., *Giving Preservation A History: Histories of Historic Preservation in the United States* (New York: Routledge, 2003); Anthony C. Wood, *Preserving New York: Winning the Right to Protect a City's Landmarks* (New York: Routledge, 2008); Daniel Bluestone, *Buildings, Landscapes, and Memory: Case Studies in Historic Preservation* (New York: W.W. Norton & Co., 2011); Miles Glendinning, *The Conservation Movement: A History of Architectural Preservation* (Abingdon: Routledge, 2013); Thordis Arrhenius, *The Fragile Monument: On Conservation and Modernity* (London: Black Dog Publishing, 2013); Stephanie M. Meeks and Kevin C. Murphy, *The Past and Future City: How Historic Preservation Is Reviving America's Communities* (Washington, DC: Island Press, 2016).

[4] See for example: Log20, *Curating Architecture*, Fall 2010; Veronique Patteuw, Tom Vandeputte and Christophe Van Gerrevey, eds., *OASE88. Exhibitions. Showing and Producing Architecture* (Rotterdam: 010 publishers, 2012); Thordis Arrhenius, Mari Lending, Wallis Miller, and Jeremie McGowan, eds., *Place and Displacement: Exhibiting Architecture* (Zurich: Lars Müller, 2014); Jean-Pierre Criqui, ed., *Cahiers du Musée national d'art moderne* (Paris: Éditions du Centre Pompidou, 2014), n.129; Roberto Gigliotti, ed., *Displayed Spaces. New Means of Architecture Presentation through Exhibitions* (Leipzig: Spector Books, 2015); *Volume 44: On Display* (Amsterdam: Archis, 2015); Eeva-Liisa Pelkonen, Carson Chan, and David Tasman, *Exhibiting Architecture: A Paradox?* (New Haven: Yale School of Architecture, 2015); Sergio Figueireido, *The NAi Effect: Creating Architecture Culture* (Rotterdam: 010 publishers, 2016); Lea-Catherine Szacka, *Exhibiting the Postmodern: The 1980 Venice Architecture Biennale* (Venice: Marsilio, 2016); Zöe Ryan, *As Seen: Exhibitions that Made Architecture and Design History* (Chicago: The Art Institute of Chicago, 2017); Eeva-Liisa Pelkonen, *Exhibit A: Exhibitions that Transformed Architecture, 1948–2000* (London: Phaidon, 2018).

[5] Phyllis Lambert, a crucial player in the panorama of early architecture museum was one of the founding members of the International Council of Architecture Museum (ICAM). The creation of the Canadian Centre for Architecture (CCA) in 1979 was linked to the birth of her collection that started with a large photographic campaign carried out with British photographer Richard Pare, with the aim of documenting Montreal's threatened patrimony of gray stone buildings, following on earlier photographic missions, notably *Courthouse*. Having campaigned for the preservation of the nineteenth-century Shaughnessy House in Montreal, Lambert made it the centerpiece of a permanent home for the CCA and its collections in 1989. Over the course of the next decades preservation would frequently be an exhibition theme.

[6] Notably the detailed drawings recording ancient, medieval, and Renaissance historical monuments done by the architects associated with France's Commission des Monuments Historiques and regularly featured for international appreciation.

[7] On Charleston, see Robert R. Weyeneth, *Historic Preservation for a Living City* (Columbia: University of South Carolina Press, 2000).

[8] Weyeneth, *Historic Preservation,* 29.

[9] Weyeneth, *Historic Preservation,* 29.

[10] "Comments," follow McCormack article cited below, note 12.

[11] "The Faces of a City,' *The News and Courier* (Charles, SC), Thursday Morning, April 16, 1942, p. 4, col. 2.

[12] Helen G. McCormack, "Architectural Inventory," *The News and Courier* (Charleston, SC, Sunday April 19, 1942, p. 5, reprinting from *JSAH* 1, no. 3, July–October 1941.

[13] Charleston (SC Civic Services Committee, Samuel Gaillard Stoney, and Carolina Art Association, *This Is Charleston: A Survey of the Architectural Heritage of a Unique American City Undertaken by the Charleston Civic Services Committee* (Charleston: Carolina Art Association for the Charleston Civic Service Committee, 1944).

[14] Anthony Wood, *Preserving New York: Winning the Right to Protect a City's Landmarks* (New York: Routledge, 2008), 115.

[15] *Monuments of Manhattan: An Exhibition of Great Buildings in New York City, 1880–1918* (New York: University Club, 1954). On the show, see also the documents in the Henry Hope Reed Papers at the Avery Library, Columbia University, Box 39, Folder 12.
[16] Twenty years later Reed would consider MoMA's large-scale exhibition *The Architecture of the Ecole des Beaux-Arts,* a triumph of his campaign in favor of academic classicism and City Beautiful values. Already in the small catalogue accompanying the University Club display he insisted on the importance of the Ecole in transforming American architecture. Richard Morris Hunt's return from Paris in 1856, one hundred year past, he said, was the beginning of the transformation of New York City in "The Age of Taste" (p. 11 of scanned version, babel.hathitrust.ord/cg/pt?id=uva.x000764880&view=1up&seq=11, accessed July 6, 2021).
[17] Henry Hope Reed Jr., in *Monuments of Manhattan,* 12 (see note 15).
[18] See Kathleen Kurtz Cook, "The Creation of Independence National Historical Park and Independence Mall," Historic Preservation Thesis, University of Pennsylvania, 1989, 125, https://repository.upenn.edu/hp_theses/353.
[19] Philip Johnson letter to Judge Edwin O. Lewis, President, Independence Hall Association, Johnson's letter, September 19, 1956. Independence Hall Historic Park Archives, quoted in Cook, "The Creation of Independence National Historical Park," 127–28.
[20] Edwin O. Lewis, President, Independence Hall Association, Letter to Philip Johnson, September 25, 1956, INHP Archives, quoted in Cook, "The Creation of Independence National Historical Park," 128.
[21] Carroll L. V. Meeks Letter to Edwin Ol. Lewis, September 25, 1956, quoted in Cook, "The Creation of Independence National Historical Park," 128.
[22] Mumford, "Philadelphia=III," *The New Yorker,* April 6, 1957, p. 140.
[23] "Architecture Worth Saving," Press Release, October 5, 1958, MoMA Press release 226131.pdf. https:assets/moma.org/documents/moma_press_release_326131.
[24] See Nina Stritzler-Levine, "Curating History, Exhibiting Ideas: Henry-Russell Hitchcock and Architectural Exhibition Policy at the MoMA," in Frank Salmon, ed., *Summerson & Hitchcock: Centenary Essays on Architectural History* (Studies in British Art, 16) (New Haven: Yale University Press, 2006), 36–68.
[25] Stritzler-Levine, "Curating History, Exhibiting Ideas."
[26] "Architecture Worth Saving" published as both a detachable pamphlet (copy online Museum of Modern Art Exhibition History web site for the exhibition) and within *Architectural Forum* 108, no. 6 (June 1958): 93–119.
[27] The MoMA show's title itself found echoes, notably in Syracuse, New York, with the publication of Architecture Worth Saving in Onondaga Country of 1964, at the height of downtown Syracuse's massive urban renewal.
[28] Ada Louise Huxtable, "Heritage in Peril; Defence of Architectural Landmarks is Purpose of Museum Display," *The New York Times,* October 5, 1958, Section X, p. 11.
[29] Huxtable, "Heritage in Peril."
[30] See Barry Bergdoll, "The Museum as Advocate of Modernist Preservation: A Case Study of the Museum of Modern Art," in Ana Tostoes and Jaime Silva, eds., *Docomomo Prize at 15* (Lisbon, 2023); see also Kevin Murphy, "The Villa Savoye and the Modernist Historic Monument," *Journal of the Society of Architectural Historians* 61, no. 1 (March 2002): 68–89; and Susanna Caccia Gherardini and Carlo Olmo, *La Villa Savoye: Icona, rovina, restauro (1948–1968)* (Rome: Donzelli Editore, 2016), esp. 180–88. See also Fondation Le Corbusier, *Le Corbusier: L'oeuvre à l'épreuve de sa restauration* (Paris: Éditions de la Villette, 2017).
[31] Ways that are not immediately clear today from the mere evidence of the installation photographs of the 1975 exhibition and the lavish book, published two years later.
[32] Memo No. 34, preparatory notes for MoMA press release, April 30, 1975, MoMA archives. See also Barry Bergdoll, "Complexities and Contradictions of Post-Modernist Classicism: Notes on the Museum of Modern Art's 1975 Exhibition," *The Architecture of the Ecole des Beaux-Arts*," in Frank Salmon, ed., *The Persistence of the Classical: Essays on Architecture Presented to David Watkin* (London: Philip Wilson Publishers, 2008), 202–17.
[33] Robert Campbell, "This show is a statement," *Boston Evening Globe,* November 10, 1975. Copy in The Museum of Modern Art Archives CUR 1110.
[34] Manuela Hoelterhoff, "Escape from a World of Glass Boxes," *The Wall Street Journal,* December 2, 1975. Copy in The Museum of Modern Art Archives CUR 1110.
[35] Ada Louise Huxtable, "Beaux Arts—the Latest Avant-garde," *The New York Times Magazine,* Sunday 26 October 1975. Copy in The Museum of Modern Art Archives CUR 1110.
[36] Letter from John Barrington Bayley to Arthur Drexler, December 2, 1977, MoMA Archives, Box 315. "Dear Arthur, First the magisterial work on the Ecole which glanced at with extreme pleasure, looked in the index, found my name, and then found myself on two pages—the médallion d'honneur. I felt wonderful."

[37] Robert Venturi, "Learning the Right Lessons from the Beaux-Arts,' *Architectural Design* 49, no. 1 (1979): 23–31.
[38] Arthur Drexler, "Beaux-Arts," memorandum, 31 January 1974, Museum of Modern Arts Archives Reg. 1110.
[39] In 2014, the V&A staged an exhibition to celebrate the fortieth anniversary of *The Destruction of the Country House*.
[40] Ruth Adams, "The V&A, The Destruction of the Country House and the Creation of 'English Heritage,'" *Museum & Society* 11, no. 1 (March 2013): 1–18.
[41] Adams, "The V&A."
[42] Adams, "The V&A," 7.
[43] See https://genome.ch.bbc.co.uk/fd36182319274d5eb70701cb70f7a74c.
[44] Marcus Binney, "Spotlight on Churches," http://www.hrballiance.org.uk/wp-content/uploads/2017/04/spotlight-on-churches.pdf.
[45] "Death of Churches," *The Observer*, July 17, 1977, 26.
[46] Binney, "Spotlight on Churches," 66.
[47] Patrick O'Donovan, "Saving Surplus Churches," *The Observer*, August 28, 1977, 7.
[48] In reality, a first exhibition of architecture had been organised in 1968 when Carlo Scarpa curated *Linee della ricerca contemporanea: Dall'informale alle nuove strutture*, a show presented in the frame of the International Art Exhibition of the Biennale and bringing together within a single space laid out by Scarpa himself the work of artists, photographers, set designers, graphic designers, ceramists and architects in order to achieve that integration between the various artistic practices.
[49] "Il concorso vuole più che progetti reali innescare un processo che possa trarre considerazioni generali sul rapporto creatività collettiva e immagine della città, quindi non e riservato a particolare categorie di operatori culturali e i suoi prodotti saranno presentati in una mostra e con una pubblicazione.' Gae Aulenti, 'Diteci come sfruttare il Molino Stucky," *Il Mondo*, Milan, April 17, 1975.
[50] Francesco Dorigo, "Proposte per il Mulino Stucky," *L'Osservatore Romano*, Citta del Vaticano, Setptember 23, 1975.
[51] Tommaso Trini, "Progetti per distruggere il Molino da Salvare," *Corriere della Sera*, September 21, 1975. The group conducted an inquiry in Corte dei Cordami on the Giudecca Island from May 22 to June 5, 1975.
[52] Tommaso Trini, "Progetti per distruggere il Molino da Salvare," *Corriere della Sera*, September 21, 1975.
[53] Jean-Jacques Larrochelle, "Cent ans de loi sur le patrimoine, dix rates," *Le Monde*, September 13, 2013.
[54] Sabine Marchand, "Venise fait appel au public pour rénover un de ses quartiers," *Le Monde*, August 27, 1975.
[55] See Lea-Catherine Szacka, *Exhibiting the Postmodern: The 1980 Venice Architecture Biennale* (Venice: Marsilio, 2016).
[56] Bruno Alfieri in *Giornale di Bergamo* wrote that part of the Biennale would have taken place in the Molino Stucky—we now know this never happened. Bruno Alfieri, "Venezia maschio-femmina," *Giornale di Bergamo*, April 22, 1975.

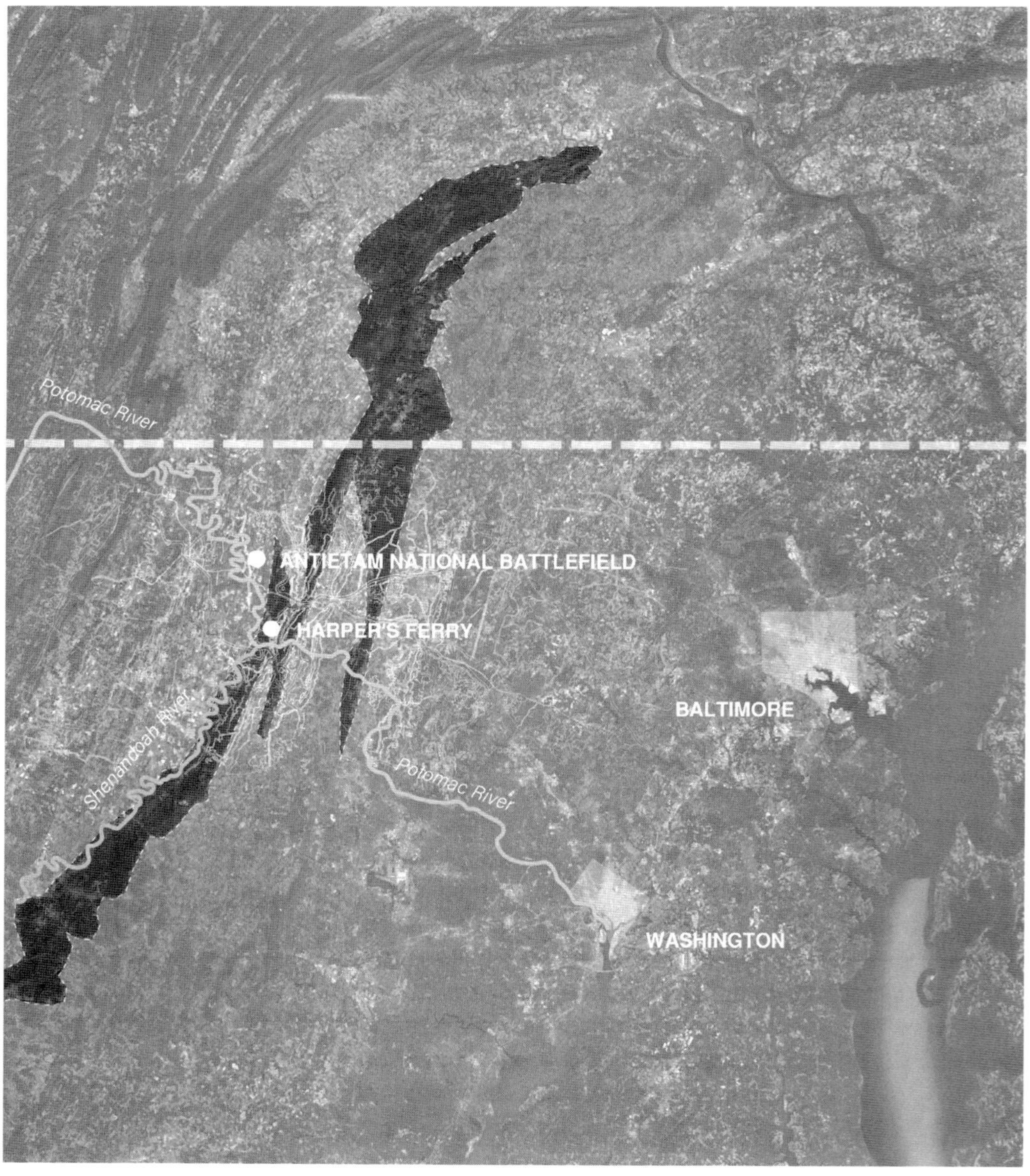

Figure 1. Map of Abolitionist Landscape. By author.

Jeffrey Hogrefe

The Abolitionist Landscape Project

A transit of Venus across the sun is visible from the earth every one hundred and twenty years. In 1761, the celestial event assembled over one hundred astronomers with improved telescopes to map the transit around the globe so as to determine for the first time the distance between celestial bodies in the Milky Way galaxy.[1] For builders of European empire, the transit of Venus introduced the concept of the global, which led to a scientific justification resulting in the appropriation of indigenous places in the Pacific, Asia, Africa, and Western Hemisphere based on the celestial coordinates that lined up with the earth. Centered on the sun, which "never set on the British Empire," empire building fits in nicely with the transit of Venus and the subsequent measurement of the longitudinal Mason–Dixon Line that eventually came to divide north and south, free and slave, in the United States. The excavation of the Mason–Dixon Line by taking down trees and destroying native pathways was consistent with the colonial project of disrupting the movement of the Indigenous population.[2] The event of the line reinforced the Enlightenment privileging of the universal and global for settler colonists. Emboldened by philosophical ideals of civilization, the Mason–Dixon project acquired extensive property that was mapped with the new technologies that provided a rational and scientific precision for the establishment of the American colonies in the time and space continuum of the removal of the Indigenous peoples and subjugation and importation of African slaves.[3]

What I have come to know as the Abolitionist Landscape Project is tightly bounded by the Mason–Dixon Line, the Enlightenment project in cartographic certainty that resides in the sign of "Dixie" and signifier of Dixie in the United States National Park Service (NPS) monuments in Harpers Ferry and Antietam. Innovative surveying equipment for the first time resulted in a line that followed the circumference of the earth.[4] It could be said that the circumference of the earth was asked to conspire with Empire in the administrative logics of slavery, since the Mason–Dixon Line—over two hundred miles in length—became a storied destination for freedom on the Underground Railroad. By the time of the Civil War the indigenous population of the Mason–Dixon Line and Potomac River Valley was largely decimated by the violence perpetrated by the logics of colonial and national administration that financed the tree

Future Anterior
Volume XX, Numbers 1–2
Summer / Winter 2023

consuming machines deployed by Charles Mason and Jeremiah Dixon. As the direct descendant of a Shawnee grandmother and abolitionist newspaper publisher grandfather—distinctly anti-slavery forces in the area—I came into the Abolitionist Landscape Project slowly over time as the historical memory of my past and that of the landscape in which the project is situated came into focus through intensive study in the archive and participation in land based ceremonial practices. These ceremonies reintroduced indigenous traditions to the landscape through the intercession of Oglala Lakota practitioners who rhizomatically emerged, after a period of hundreds of years, in the Potomac River Valley from Pine Ridge Reservation in South Dakota over a thousand miles to the west.[5]

The Abolitionist Landscape Project is a haunting of the landscape that lives as an archive of personal experiences, historical documents, and maps, and a syllabus of critical ethnography to propose a new, intergenerational space for possible utopian futures. Through creative practices in Afrosurrealism, Abolitionist and Landscape are joined together in an unlikely neologism that defines the project, which sets out to uncover the underlying cultural formations in the landscape that led to such an important event as the abolition of slavery. Afrosurrealism repositions Blackness and Indigeneity as central to Surrealism to result in "an entirely different world connected organically to this one," through topological deformations of the figure of the place.[6] A topology of the way ideas are organized is a smooth surface that can be altered for the purposes of a continuous transformation to show, in this case, the time-space continuum of landscape, slavery, Indigenous removal, and abolition. Landscape does not simply function as decorative background, it opens up the possibility of thinking about the production of space as unfinished, resulting in a poetics of space where abolition emerges in the landscape as a potent political and aesthetic force through critical practices in Afrosurrealism. Abolition and landscape come together to reveal and engage in a past that has been erased from view through governmental representation, stressing the existential importance of the politics of space and place, and embodying the theme of intergenerational continuity central to Afrosurrealism utopianism.

My grandfather introduced me to the concept of the abolitionist landscape when he drove me one night from Washington, DC, where we had been visiting the sites of the capital, to witness the junction of the rivers at Harpers Ferry. The contrast of the gleaming white marble monuments of the nation's capital and the sublime beauty of the soft, graceful mountains as they caressed the intersection of the Potomac and Shenandoah rivers, and the story of our family's activities in the Underground Railroad, lodged in my mind. Potomac is the Algonquin word for "place where transactions take place." Shenandoah translates as "daughter of the stars." My grandfather was proud to say that he was a descendant of Shawnee people who harbored escaped slaves and an abolitionist newspaper publisher. Yet for me it was as if the landscape that night was opened to reveal another story that was difficult for me to piece together out of the fragments of our family's past.

Located seventy miles west of Washington, DC, in the southern half of the United States on the upland border of the Mason–Dixon Line as it bisects the Appalachian Mountains—in this contested landscape the U.S. National Park Service (NPS) maintains two monuments: Harpers Ferry National Monument, the site of John Brown's revolutionary act of 1859, and Antietam National Battlefield, the site of the Civil War battle that led to the 1863 Emancipation Proclamation granting freedom to over four million enslaved laborers (Figure 1). The Indigenous and Black American voices that inform the contested landscape have been essentially silenced as a result of the revisionist histories under the direction of the NPS in the service of structural white supremacy. This governmental design and maintenance of historic monuments has had the effect of freezing past events in crystalline moments that privilege the universalist image of the white soldier and white slave owners in a simulacrum, a representational imaginary of an idealized past.

Let us be clear that the underlying cause of the Civil War was the abolition of slavery, and for the purposes of this study that we are examining what Saidiya Hartman refers to as the "afterlife of slavery,"[7] a structural economy that is still deeply embedded in the national consciousness as exemplified by the ways in which histories are told in official exhibitions. In fact, the establishment of a national culture was seriously compromised by the ongoing debate over slavery that consumed the government in the years leading up to the Civil War, and still afterward in a succession of Jim Crow segregation, red lining, urban renewal, neighborhood gentrification, the ongoing war on drugs/crime, escalation of police brutality, and circulation of images that denigrate Black people.

In 1963 and 1966 the National Park Service brought together the two key racialized moments in the history of the US principally as a stage for the performance of patriotism and white supremacy that obscure the Black and Indigenous histories, a program consistent with other federal projects in the middle of the twentieth century such as the construction of interstate highways that cut through Black enclaves.[8] Carefully choreographed reenactments convey the message that the soldiers on both sides are "noble, committed to the same ideology, and united by the experience of the battle."[9] A quarter of a million people visit the sites each year, most of them white people from the South even though a significant Black population lives only an hour and a half drive in Baltimore and Washington, D.C. (Figures 2, 3).[10] Individual rangers, various new educational brochures and renovations attempt to present a nuanced position of the sites. Overall, the exhibitions create a usable past for a white constituency by relegating the Black and Indigenous stories to the background as components in a white history. This whitewashed interpretation of the past is in keeping with the standard practice of the NPS of evacuating Indigenous presence to present an empty continent that is ready for white settlement, a trope that is still evident in these sites although other recent NPS exhibitions foreground the Indigenous past.[11] Warfare is the leitmotif of these memorials that have been constructed out of the fabric of the past into shining displays, which can be viewed by anyone who cares to consider the effect of the Civil War on the landscape of the Potomac River Valley.

Harpers Ferry National Park presents, "African American," as part of its mission; a single building among about ten buildings tells the story of the Black American's presence in the town. In 2019, at the seventy-fifth anniversary of the national monument out of the twenty-seven events only two were related to Black American history: one, on the Green Book, which published lodging and food establishments that would serve Blacks during segregation; the other, a jazz concert featuring a former faculty member at Storer College as a performer.[12] Storer College was opened in 1866 to educate formerly enslaved laborers and closed in 1955 as a result of the Brown versus Board of Education decision that declared that segregated education was unconstitutional. With the closing of the school, the significant Black American community of Harpers Ferry declined precipitously. Eventually, the NPS purchased the main campus of the school. The orientation of the exhibitions to a white audience has compromised the desire of some of the staff and local residents to introduce presentations of the African American and Indigenous histories. Although the NPS conducted an ethnography in 2017 and has reinterpreted Antietam Battlefield to show the important role of Black soldiers in the Civil War, the orientation of the exhibits toward a white audience has compromised the presentation of a full picture of the Black experience in the Potomac River Valley. Attempts by the NPS to include a Black perspective overly emphasize the role that Blacks played in the militarization of the landscape instead of as a distinct culture forged within a history of racial violence and developed out of a history of resistance. Visitors might conclude from the display that the Union won the Civil War due to the fighting prowess of Black soldiers without considering the legacy of the

Figure 2. John Brown's Fort. Harpers Ferry National Monument. NPS Photo/Autumn Cook.

Figure 3. Visitor's Center Antietam National Battlefield. NPS Photo.

preceding two hundred years of brutal subjugation that have been followed by ongoing state and extra-state persecution and extermination—an important historical and cultural context that is missing from the exhibition's sole focus on warfare.

The strategic location of the United States Arsenal at Harpers Ferry, as the holding place for arms and ammunition for the southern half of the US, brought John Brown to the river town to stage a revolutionary act to arm an insurrection of enslaved laborers in what he referred to as the "Great Black Way" of the southern slave plantations (Figure 4).[13] The bravado of the revolutionary's rhetorical performance contributed significantly to the justification for the Civil War that ended slavery. During the war, newly emancipated enslaved laborers flooded into Harpers Ferry to camp around "John Brown's fort," the thick-walled, squat, red brick classical fire engine house that Brown and his followers seized for a day and a half in 1859. In the words of W. E. B. Du Bois, as a result of its symbolic role, Harpers Ferry acquired the status of "hallowed ground," for the Black American, resulting in annual political celebrations of Black people at "John Brown's Fort."[14]

Today, "John Brown's Fort," relegated to an ancillary position with its back facing the recreated town, is no longer the site for annual pilgrimages of Black American people and allies; instead, it has been the site of a Ku Klux Klan rally and Park volunteers who interpret Brown's legacy as terrorism.[15] The story of slavery in the Harpers Ferry National Monument Visitor's Center lives in a panorama that depicts a graphic metaphor of a tornado that swept up from the Deep South to bring ruin to the small white town instead of as a force that swept through the Black families who were sold to the plantations in the Deep South.[16] The story of the enslaved people in Maryland and Virginia who were forced to produce offspring to be sold in the growing market of cotton and sugar plantations in the Deep South is known as "the half not told," further complicating the traumatic history of sexual violence against Black Americans.[17] The inspiration for the panorama is Thomas Jefferson's comment on slavery on the occasion of the Missouri Compromise of 1820, which legalized slavery in Missouri: "All do not see the speck on the horizon which is to burst upon us like a tornado."[18] This myopic position could only have been presented by a slave owner; Clearly, to the enslaved laborer suffering the pain of chattel bondage, slavery was more than a speck on the horizon.

To Harpers Ferry's sacred place for the Black American, Antietam is a touchstone for the "Lost Cause," a white supremacist ideology that reinforces the belief that the Civil War should have ended with a southern victory, a resurgent force in the era of white nationalism.[19] Matthew Brady's photographs of the battle amply document the war dead in gruesome floor to ceiling panels in the visitor's center to underscore the loss of white lives. Antietam was not only the site of the 1862 Civil War battle that inspired Abraham Lincoln to issue the Emancipation Proclamation in 1863. Moreover, central to the battle was the position of the Dunkers Church, a squat wood frame vernacular structure which was a site of a prayer vigil for a cessation of the fighting by the abolitionist congregation.[20] Yet, the focus of the official US government representation is upon warfare.

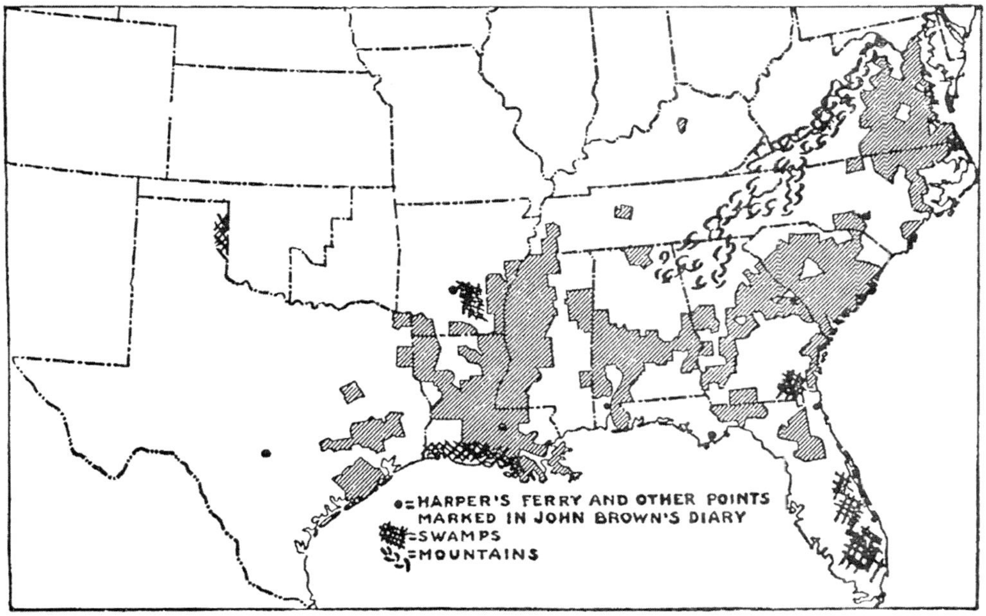

Map Showing the Great Black Way

Figure 4. Great Black Way map in W. E. Burghardt Du Bois. John Brown. (New York: International Publisher, 1909–1969), 105–6.

The sites of entanglement in the mediated experience of the NPS led me to create the Abolitionist Landscape Project, which in turn is inspired by Afrosurrealism because it incorporates Asiatic, Indigenous and African influences in pursuit of liberation from the economic forces that reinforce the militarization of landscape. Afrosurrealism offers a possible rupture in the landscape to allow the space for utopian possibilities to emerge in the Potomac River Valley through a deformation of the figure of the monument to reveal an alternative to the present (Figure 5).

In an analysis of the underlying structural meaning of monuments, Henri Lefebvre points out in *The Production of Space* that monuments constitute "the strong points, nexuses or anchors of a network of webs."[21] that are regulated by social, symbolic, and political forces. A monumental work is not fixed or static, it is dynamic and fluid. Within the network, "a monumental work . . . has a horizon of meanings; a specific or indefinite multiplicity of meanings, a shifting hierarchy in which now one, now another meaning comes momentarily to the fore, by means of—and for the sake of—a particular action."[22]

Lefebvre's theory that meaning in a monumental space can shift for a particular action is critical to the mapping operation of the Abolitionist Landscape Project. The project proposes that the human capacity to monumentalize, supported by symbolic formations in the battlefields and historic towns of the Civil War, can be acted on and against by the human capacity to locate interpretative practices focusing on the act

Figure 5. U.S. governmental monuments entangled with vines in the Anthropocene. By author.

of walking as the singular origin of all meaning and walkers as co-creators of the landscape in time and space. [23] Through interpretive, self-referential, and procedural walking practices, the Abolitionist Landscape Project assembles an archive of alternative histories and performances as a counter-monument to the NPS's interpretation of sites that privilege the image of the white soldier and white slave owners in an imaginary representation of a past that never existed. The Afrosurrealist interpretation embedded in the project reorders, in uncanny juxtapositions, the events and objects that contain memories of the Indigenous and Black American for an alternative to the presentation of the NPS. The military grounds of Antietam and Harpers Ferry seem to appear algorithmically in a tightly bound knot with the Mason–Dixon Line as it cuts across the paths that led the Indigenous in and out of the Potomac River Valley, and formerly enslaved laborers into freedom in the North. Instead of celebrating the abolition of slavery, the monuments reproduce the trauma of slavery and displaced Indigeneity in their exclusionary interpretations.

Afrosurrealism, an aesthetic practice that is concerned with deformation of the figure as it locates an imaginary world that is living in concert with the real world, alters the way that the present moment is experienced in the violent history of people. As fashioned by Amiri Baraka, Afrosurrealism defines an approach to literary fabulation that is found in the writing of historians and literary figures such as Saidiya Hartman, Katherine McKittrick, Toni Morrison, and Zora Neale Hurston.[24] Per Baraka: "Stories of real life, now or whenever, constructed in weirdness and poetry in which the contemporaneity of essential themes is clear."[25] As it seeks to unravel and reorder new imaginary potential for the immanent every day and the ordinary, Afrosurrealism offers a possible rupture in the text of the place of Harpers Ferry and Antietam to allow the space of Black Americans and the Indigenous Americans to emerge in the Potomac River Valley.

Africa is latent in the cultural landscape of the United States; the cultural filaments of Africa were removed and carried to the continent by the millions of enslaved laborers whose past lives are still present in the slave labor camps, and where the millions of formerly enslaved have been and are still crowded into substandard housing in the degradation of the "slum/ghetto," of American cities.[26] "The mystic spell of Africa is and ever was over all America,"[27] writes W. E. B. Du Bois. Rejecting all forms of racism, Afrosurrealism emphasizes the value of excess and the everyday and the imaginary, an unlikely juxtaposition of the phenomenon in the unconscious as a productive place of transformation from the networks that create and maintain the monuments in the landscape. The NPS functions to shore up capitalist and neocolonial state. Afrosurrealism "presupposes that beyond this visible world, there is an invisible world striving to manifest, and it is our job to uncover it."[28]

You will see here an Afrosurrealist mapping of a section of the Antietam Battlefield (Figures 6, 7)—the path between the obelisk that was erected to honor the civil war soldiers from New York State and the Dunkers Church. What interested me in creating this walk was the relationship between the monument and the Dunker's Church, which is located within a short walk away from the Obelisk. When mapping the site, it was the space in between the two that interested me in my walk, and the way that that space affected the inside of the church. The phallic symbol of the monument appeared to provide a blunt force to the squat sheltering warm space of the church. The masculine space of the battlefield, with its marble shafts and observation towers, detailed maps and display cases of armaments and photographs of the war casualties, actively recreates the battle in a visitor's mind. From a psychoanalytic point of view, the gaze is on the masculine and the valor and courage of the soldiers—and the phallic symbol inherent in the monument.

The "Dunkers'" were German Baptist Brethren, named for practicing complete immersion during baptism. Water flows

Figure 6. Map of walk taken by author at Antietam National Battlefield. By author.

Figure 7. Collage of walk taken by author at Antietam National Battlefield. By author.

through the site in the memory of the immersive practices of the Dunkers and the Antietam Creek, which empties into the Potomac River a few miles south. Antietam translates from Algonquin to English as swift water. Water is central to the experience of the history of the Middle Passage during the period of Transatlantic slave trading and the immersive experiences of baptism. Water is heavy and obdurate, swift and flowing, cleansing and healing. Writes Tiffany Lethabo King: "At the shoal (and shore)—or the in- between space—the White cartographic subject is a byproduct of Black and Indigenous pressure or friction from the outside."[29]

During the time inside the church I began to think about containment, isolation, and histories of the abolition of slavery that have been erased from the battlefield site by the deliberate reordering of events and the objects that contain the white memory of the conflict. Lost in the thoughts about containment and isolation that came to me as I sat in the church, I observed that most of the visitors to the site were unprepared to utilize the space of the structure for a lasting experience. Most visitors only remained in the church for one second—I timed them. This led to new thoughts about the abolition of slavery and what it means to be contained and isolated and then set free without any consideration for the passage that must be taken between slavery and freedom. Perhaps the reason that people are reluctant to utilize the space for reflection of the memory of the abolition of slavery is that the memory of the containment of the slave in the hidden passageways that held the enslaved body is simply too great to bear. This led me to think about Henry Box Brown, a formerly enslaved African who shipped himself out of slavery in a box that measured three feet by two feet, labeled with a sign that read "This Side Up With Care" stenciled on the baize lined wooden container.[30]

There are multiple readings of the same place in a space of poetic figuration. Memory ultimately resides in the land, which has agency. History repeats itself in the place where it is recorded. Box Brown was never at the Antietam Battlefield; he was in Richmond and moved by rail for twenty-seven hours in a small container to Philadelphia.[31] By enacting the layers on the ground, Box Brown's spirit was and still is in Antietam as much as my ancestors, the vanquished Indigenous people, and the self-emancipated enslaved laborer who was transported through the woods in the cold dark winter as mysteriously as Brown's body moved through the United States Postal Service without detection. Henry Box Brown appears to fly over Antietam the way that Black spirituals imagine the chariot that swings low and high—a phantasmagorical figure revealing the hidden structures of labor erased from the site.

Conceived as a template for participants to navigate their own personal interests through walking and other creative practices, the goal of the Abolitionist Landscape Project is to act in and around the official US governmental monuments as counter monuments as they begin to fall into decay in the post Anthropocene. I imagine a day when these US government monuments and ersatz historic structures will become entangled with vines like the old Victorian sections of Bombay and walkers will have to hack their way through the overgrowth. In this way, multiple engagements with the entangled sites of governance can take place, disclosing the underlying tensions and connections that give shape to the worlds of our present. Building on sites of memory, trauma, racialized experience, and governmental representation, the Abolitionist Landscape Project addresses the scale of the bounded sites and spaces as well as the broader networks and frameworks in which the landscape is situated. For Katherine McKittrick, poetics of landscape constitute narrative acts, delineating a "relationship with the land, one that is even more threatened because the community is alienated from the land. . . . Describing the landscape is not enough. The individual, the community, the land are inextricable in the process of creating history."[32] Acting as a counterirritant to the militarization of landscape by proposing that the landscape is the singular origin of all meanings, walkers are the co-creators of landscape in time and space, relaxing a tightly bound landscape in an intergenerationally shared experience of space.

Biography

Jeffrey Hogrefe is Professor of Humanities and Media Studies, co-founder of the Architecture Writing Program, and affiliate faculty in the graduate program in Landscape Architecture at Pratt Institute in Brooklyn, NY. As an Oglala Lakota Sundance person, he is a transdisciplinary scholar and creative practitioner who works on a transformative pedagogy in aesthetics and politics at the intersection of the built, imagined, and found environment. Hogrefe is the coeditor of *In Search of African American Space Redressing Racism* (Lars Muller, 2020), a recipient of the 2020 ARCC Book Award and the Pratt Institute Research Recognition Award. His research is recognized by several grants from the Graham Foundation for Advanced Studies in the Fine Arts, as well as the U.S. Department of Education, and the Taconic Foundation.

Acknowledgments

This article is an excerpt of a book-length project of the same title. The theory and practice presented here is the result of the encouragement and contributions of many people over many years. I'd like to especially thank my wife, the artist Susan Weller, for accompanying me to the Potomac River Valley for collaboratives; Daniel Abrahamson and Jonah Rowen, for their valuable suggestions on the panel they chaired at the Society of Architectural Historians' annual meeting in Pittsburgh; Thaisa Way, for her insightful suggestions at the Garden and Landscape seminar at Harvard University's Dumbarton Oaks program; Onaje Muid, for his encouragment at the social practice seminar he conducted at Columbia University; and Scott Ruff, for a generous invitation to introduce Afrosurrealism to his students at an advanced design studio at Yale University.

Notes

[1] Jodi Byrd, *Transit of Empire: Indigenous Critiques of Colonialism* (Minneapolis: University of Minnesota Press, 2011), 1–5.

[2] In 1750, Thomas Harper established a ferry to cross the Potomac River at a time when the colonial governor of Virginia decreed the removal of the native population to the headwaters of the rivers. Annual floods brought evidence of the upstream settlements to the colonists; The flooding of the rivers has complicated the archaeology for a pre-conquest narrative. https://www.nps.gov/hafe/index.htm

Moreover, in 1763, the colonial governor of Virginia urged a cessation of the abolitionist practice of aiding self-emancipated slaves among Indian tribes. During the same period, a battle was staged by the colonial governors of Maryland and Virginia between the Catawba from the south and the Delaware from the north in a prelude to the Civil War.

Woody Holton, *Forced Founders Indians, Debtors, Slaves & the Making of the American Revolution in Virginia* (Chapel Hill: University of North Carolina Press, 1991), 139. https://www.nps.gov/hafe/index.htm https://www.nps.gov/anti/index.htm

[3] Byrd, *Transit of Empire Indigenous Critiques of Colonialism,* 1–5.

[4] Adam Lifshey, "Bordering the Subjunctive in Thomas Pynchon's Mason & Dixon," *Journal X* 9, no. 1 (2004): 11–15.

[5] Conversations with Reed Brown Sr. and Reed Brown Jr. in March 2008.

[6] Amiri Baraka, "Henry Dumas Afro-Surreal Expressionist," *Black American Literature Forum* 22, no. 2, Henry Dumas Issue (Summer 1988): 164–66.

[7] Saidiya Hartman, *Scenes of Subjection: Terror, Slavery and Self Making in Nineteenth Century America* (New York: Oxford University Press, 1997), 75. Hartman defines the "afterlife of slavery" as, "the still unfolding narrative of captivity, dispossession, and domination that engenders the Black subject in the Americas."

[8] Interstate highways that cut through Black enclaves has been documented in many sources, notably in Liam Dillon and Ben Poston, "The Racist History of America's Interstate Highway Boom," *LA Times,* November 11, 2021, https://www.latimes.com/homeless-housing/story/2021-11-11/the-racist-history-of-americas-interstate-highway-boom.

[9] Denise D. Meringolo, *Museums, Monuments, and National Parks Toward a New Genealogy of Public History* (Amherst: University of Massachusetts Press, 2012), 89.

[10] See Megan Bailey, An Ethnographic Overview and Assessment: Harper's Ferry National Historical Park (National Park Service, 2017), https://npshistory.com/publications/hafe/eoa.

[11] Meringolo, *Museums, Monuments, and National,* 54.

[12] The relevant details of the cited events at the 75th anniversary are found in the USNPS digital publication, "75th Anniversary of Harpers Ferry National Park," Harpers Ferry National Park in partnership with the Harpers Ferry Park Association, 2019. https://www.nps.gov/hafe/planyourvisit/harpersferry75.htm

[14] Andrew W. Kahrl, "The Political Work of Leisure Class, Recreation and African American Commemoration at Harpers Ferry, West Virginia, 1881–1931." Journal of Social History 42, no. 1 (Fall 2008): 57–77.

[15] Courtland Milloy, "Hate Is Always in Style," October 17, 2006, The Washington Post. https://www.washingtonpost.com/archive/local/2006/10/18/hate-is-always-in-style-at-a-gathering-of-the-klan/9faa4068-8fcf-4e19-b38f-25e4d5c8177c/

[16] See "tornado," jpeg.

[17] Edward E. Baptist, *The Half Has Never Been Told Slavery and the Making of American Capitalism* (New York: Basic Books, 2014), xii–xxiv.

[18] The Thomas Jefferson Papers at the Library of Congress: Series 1: General Correspondence. 1651 to 1827. See "Slavery's Storm," exhibited at John Brown Museum, Harpers Ferry National Historic Park.

[19] Jon D. Bohland, "A Lost Cause Found: Vestiges of Old South Memory in the Shenandoah Valley of Virginia," PhD diss., Virginia Polytechnic Institute and State University, 2006.

[20] "Slavery and Emancipation in Sharpsburg, Maryland," Antietam National Battlefiled, National Park Service, https://www.nps.gov/anti/learn/historyculture/slavery-and-emancipation-in-sharpsburg.htm

[21] Henri Lefebvre, *The Production of Space* [1974], trans. Donald Nicholson-Smith. (Oxford: Blackwell Publishing, 1991), 222–23.

[22] Lefebvre, *The Production of Space,* 222–23.

[23] Lefebvre, *The Production of Space,* 222–23.

[24] First coined by Amiri Baraka, Afro-surrealism is a transhistorical practice in the everyday for the African American. D. Scott Miller, "Call It Afro-Surrealism," 48hills 43, no. 34, May 19, 2009, http://48hills.org/sfbgarchive/2009/05/19/call-it-afro-surreal/.

[25] Baraka, "Henry Dumas Afro-Surreal Expressionist," 164–66.

[26] In the epigraph of *Beloved,* Toni Morrison poses "Sixty Million and More" to the question of the number of descendants of the slave subject in the United States. Toni Morrison, *Beloved* (New York: Random House, 1987), epigraph.

[27] W. E. B. Du Bois, *John Brown* (New York: International Publisher, 1969), 1.

[28] D. Scot Miller "The Afrosurreal Manifesto: A Living Document," Open Space SFMOMA November 29, 2016, https://openspace.sfmoma.org/2016/11/the-afrosurreal-manifesto-a-living-document/.
[29] Tiffany Lethabo King, *The Black Shoals: Offshore Formations of Black and Indigenous Studies* (Durham: Duke University Press, 2019), 78.
[30] Henry Brown, *Narrative of the Life of Henry Box Brown Written by Himself* (New York: Oxford University Press, 2002), xiii.
[31] Brown, *Narrative of Henry Box Brown,* xi.
[32] Katherine McKittrick, *Demonic Ground: Black Women and the Cartographies of Struggle* (Minneapolis: University of Minnesota Press, 1997), xxii; Edouard Glissant, *Caribbean Discourse* (Charlottesville: University of Virginia Press, 1989.), 105.

Figure 1. The arrival of employees at the Baťa factory in Baťovany. Státní okresní archiv Zlín (State District Archive Zlin), Sbírka fotografií Zlín, obálka č. 15125, poř. č. 2.

Nina Bartošová, Barbora Vacková, and Veronika Rypák Vaňo

From Past to Future

The Walking Phenomenon in the Identity of Partizánske/Baťovany

The industrial settlements that the Baťa company built on several continents around the world are a unique example of the application of an idea inspired by period concepts of the ideal city, which gradually took shape in the Moravian city of Zlín (then in interwar Czechoslovakia, now the Czech Republic), where the company was based. These "satellites" of Zlín, as they were called, were characterized not only by similar urban planning principles, but also by specific architecture. Partizánske—originally Baťovany—was founded as one of the company's satellites in Western Slovakia just before the beginning of World War II. The war, apart from putting Partizánske on the other side border from Zlín, caused the town's final form to deviate from the original ideas. Even in reunified Czechoslovakia after the war, the incoming Communist Party was not interested in returning to the Baťa aesthetic, which it condemned as an undesirable symbol of capitalism. It was only after its collapse in 1989—followed shortly thereafter by the dissolution of Czechoslovakia—that interest in what Baťa had built began to increase in both countries.

Partizánske is considered to be the "Slovak Zlín,"[1] but there is another difference between the two cities in that while the state historic preservation policies were successfully introduced in Zlín, this is not the case in Partizánske.[2] In this text we argue that precisely because the intensity of the characteristic Baťa architecture is weaker in contemporary Partizánske than in Zlín, it is appropriate to reconsider the aspects on which historic preservation is based. In addition to values directly related to the preserved material essence of the buildings, it is important that theoretical foundations integrate the knowledge of how the values of the city are perceived by the inhabitants themselves. More than how they conceptualize them, their shared on-the-ground experience of the city's space can be a precursor to setting a specific preservation policy. This suggests greater significance can be given to the well-known fact that Partizánske was conceived as a pedestrian city, and the act of walking elevated to become a tool for preserving the original urbanism.

The character of the research made it important to link the knowledge of an architect dealing with the theory of historic preservation of twentieth-century architecture (N. Bartošová) with a sociologist who has long been working on Zlín (B. Vacková).[3]

Future Anterior
Volume XX, Numbers 1–2
Summer / Winter 2023

They were complemented by an architect / PhD candidate (V. Rypák Vaňo), aiming to identify what preservation strategies might be applicable in Partizánske, her native city. Although there was some preexisting understanding of the problem on both sides—of both the current theory of historic preservation and the role the discipline of sociology can play in this issue—it was only the process of applying the chosen sociological method of the *focus group*, proposed and led entirely by the sociologist, that made it possible to collect such data from the participants as would not bias their responses with expectations primarily from the perspective of historic preservation theory. However, it was only the subsequent transdisciplinary analysis of the focus group recordings that facilitated a shift from the—initially assumed—static-oriented experience of the city space to dynamically experiencing it through the act of walking.

The text is divided into five parts. Since we argue that the need for a different approach to the existing heritage in Partizánske is due to aspects that distinguish Partizánske from Zlín, the first part starts with a brief characterization of the Baťa cities' values, their urbanism and architecture, in order to be able to explain later the ways Partizánske has deviated from these features. Explaining the history of Partizánske in the second part and its influence on the character of the town can help to understand why the Baťa heritage is less evident here today, which also makes applying the traditional approach of historic preservation unlikely. Following on from this, the third section introduces theories of alternative approaches that deepen understanding of heritage-making processes, including those inspired by phenomenology and thus bodily experience. These specifically led us to the decision to use the sociological method of focus groups in our research. The fourth section presents the course of the focus group, while what follows in the fifth section discusses the aspect of walking in more detail.

1. Urban Planning and Architecture of the Baťa Company

The urban design of Zlín and its subsequent satellites was based on modernist city planning, with individual functions defining separate zones. However, the Baťa construction department likewise took into consideration rational and maximally economical solutions, in terms of time as well as financial expenses. In production halls the pathways were to be as short as possible, and problems large and small to be resolved over the telephone. This aspect of the factory area also held for the town as a whole: it was planned with a logical flow among individual parts, easily accessible (by river, rail, and road), with getting around within to be as simple as could be. In the interwar period Baťa shoe production went multinational, attracting attention not only through how it applied its own version of organizing work based on the Ford-Taylor model,[4] but also being notable in the scope and form in which the Baťa company gradually built its many production sites, referred to as satellites—as smaller versions of Zlín—in Europe, North America, and other continents.

Tomáš Baťa, who headed the enterprise from 1908 to 1932, enriched by his personal work experience in the United States,[5] realized that the specific architectural and urban form to embody his vision would have to be entrusted to proficient architects. He recruited some externally—Le Corbusier himself was at Zlín for a short time—but many more worked within the company's construction department, which played a key part in creating the Baťa aesthetic. Baťa's striving for efficiency was also reflected in the architecture, which is characterized by standardization, typification, and the use of the 6.15m × 6.15m module for all factory buildings as well as amenities—wherever the structure consisted of a reinforced concrete skeleton.[6] At the same time, concrete elements were legible on the facade and complemented by red brickwork. The size of the window openings was adapted to the individual buildings' functions. For housing the preference was for individual houses, but these were also typified, designed in several variations as a single house or a duplex, situated in unfenced green areas.

How the towns were to look grew out of years of Zlín urban planning, and deliberation on an industrial town's optimal form, based on factors we might call the enterprise's manufacturing and personnel needs. Yet the gradually formed principles in the theory of the ideal industrial town related not simply to the company's functioning. The theory included topics of social policy (care of residents/employees, providing basic needs and services, etc.), and principles of company marketing and management (emphasizing the use of company media and of management type). The town was planned as a functional social unit whose conception went beyond aspects of the manufacturing environment. The aim was to create a complex living space for all categories of company employees, and not just factory workers.[7]

2. The Case of Partizánske/Baťovany

The characteristics of Baťa planning and architecture mentioned in the first part of the text can be found in Partizánske; but while in Zlín they dominate so strongly that even the Communist regime was not able to erase its visible traces, in Partizánske they are much less evident and thus so is the origin of the city. To a large extent, this relates to the historical context of the time when the town was founded, which allowed typical Baťa company aesthetics to be present only to a lesser extent. However, contemporary Partizánske is still valued for having applied the scheme of the ideal Baťa company town, and Slovakia's first modernist town, with methodically distinct functional zones for manufacture, housing, services, and recreation based on the masterplan designed by the Czech architect Jiří Voženílek.[8] This is why previous efforts to enforce historic preservation policies were based mainly on emphasizing aspects of similarity to Zlín, as this is where the original masterplan came from.[9] The aim of this part is not only to describe how Partizánske/Baťovany developed, but also to point out that preservation strategies should take into account what makes it specific.

Baťovany was constructed in August 1938 in the Upper Nitra region in Slovakia. This initially related to the Czechoslovak government's plan to industrialize what was then a mostly agricultural Slovak country, as a response to the great economic crisis of the early 1930s.[10] Unlike Zlín, the advantage was that Baťovany lacked historical structure to which the newly designed urban plan had to adjust. Where most of the urban utopias in the early twentieth century were a reaction to large city industrialization, where car transport was essential (Garnier, Hilberseimer, Le Corbusier, F. L. Wright),[11] in the Baťa satellites the company could focus on foot traffic, because the whole conception grew from the anticipated total number of workers—in Baťovany something between 5,000 and 15,000 residents.[12]

Therefore, walking as the preferred way of getting around determined Baťovany's masterplan. Its composition centered on the pedestrian promenade from the factory area running northwest to the center of town is legible today. Beyond the green belt and the existing railway tracks that separate the factory from the rest of town,[13] the promenade proceeds to the elongated central town-square urban space, with a variety of facilities. In the original master plan, matching residential zones on both sides enfolded the linked park space detached from the square by a road. Voženílek's unusual breaking of the promenade axis at the point where it comes into the central urban space gave the town square buildings a more appropriate orientation—from northwest to southeast.[14]

Soon after, as construction work on the Baťovany began, it was marked by the events leading to the World War II. Following the Munich Agreement (September 29, 1938) Czechoslovakia was split, and Baťovany became part of the new wartime Slovak Republic, a direct client state of Germany, while the parent company in Zlín was within the Protectorate of Bohemia and Moravia. Jan Antonín Baťa, who headed the company after its founder—his half-brother Tomáš Baťa—died (1932), managed to create a mutually beneficial agreement with the Slovak

Figure 2. Aerial view of Baťovany during World War II. Courtesy of Department of Architecture, Institute of History of the Slovak Academy of Sciences.

Figure 3. Walking employees of the Baťa factory in Baťovany in 1946 and 1947 (left) and in the 1980's (right), when the factory was rebranded as Závody 29. Augusta to honor the local Partisans. Courtesy of the Vydavateľstvo Tempo, s.r.o. (Tempo Newspaper Publisher), Partizánske, Slovakia.

government, based on a promise that the Baťa company would share in developing the nation state, secured the company's free hand in doing business.[15] However, in several aspects the bond to Zlín weakened, among others J. A. Baťa definite departure, ultimately for Brazil, in May 1939, less than a year after construction started and two months before production began.

These circumstances, and the war years, affected the extent and character of construction. This appears when comparing the 1938 and 1946 plans. Where the earlier proposal almost completely projects the ideal town concept into the local context, the later version from which realization developed abandons this concept in several aspects. The most visible change is in the residential zone, southwest of the central space, where multistory apartment buildings replaced individual houses of the garden city (E. Howard) model;[16] however, the realization of individual houses in green spaces as such also materialized differently than in Zlín. The reason is that time allowed construction on only one street (Červená ulica, meaning "Red Street") of typical Baťa "cubes," with brick facing and flat roofs, before the German-influenced building law decreed more traditional architecture inspired by Italian and German patterns, with white, hipped roof houses.[17] This German-influenced tendency affected other satellites too, but for Partizánske—where it is most proliferated—it was a clear departure from the Baťa look, indeed a questioning of the original Baťa model, as architectural historian Henrieta Moravčíková comments.[18]

In comparing the master plans, another difference, this one little addressed, appears in Vladimír Karfík's Roman Catholic church—the only building successfully given legal protection.[19] It prominence in the town's central space—unseen in other towns—derives not from Baťa ideal industrial town schemes; in the 1946 plan the church's position becomes more significant, as it shows no other building transversely closing the southeast side of the square, nor any smaller structure in the first third of the park, as had figured in the 1938 plan. The church thus becomes—atypically for a Baťa scheme—the culmination of the entire central space. Albeit the Baťa Zlín construction department designed several churches the company tolerated rather than encouraged religion.[20]

Many saw it as problematic when in 1963 a high-rise panel dormitory went up at one end of the park; for almost sixty years it blocked the view of the church, until after long discussion demolition began in spring of 2020. However, residents' negative attitude to the structure was associated mostly with its symbolizing the Communist regime's arrival after Czechoslovakia's reunification after the World War II. The regime nationalized the Baťa plant, depicting J. A. Baťa as an exploitative capitalist

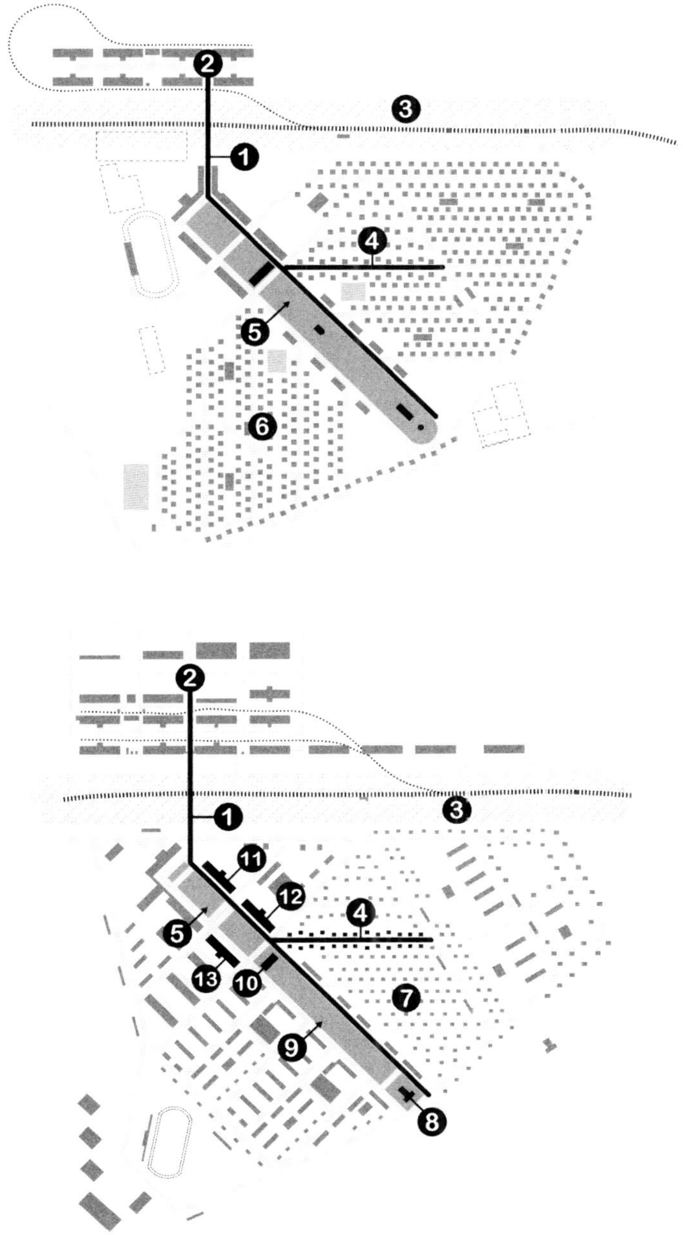

Figure 4. Representation of differences between Voženílek's master plans of Baťovaný from 1938 (top) and 1946 (bottom): 1. Pedestrian promenade, 2. Factory site, 3. Green belt, 4. Červená Street, 5. Central area, 6. Unbuilt area of individual houses, 7. Individual houses with hipped roofs, 8. Church building by Vladimír Karfík, 9. Park in the central area, 10. High-rise panel dormitory, 11. Hotel "Spoločenský dom," 12. and 13. Baťa school dormitories for young women and young men.

who moreover collaborated with the Nazi regime; the town was renamed from Baťovany to Partizánske, and the dormitory obstructed the church view, supposedly to disrupt associations with the preceding era and the undesirable church. Therefore, its renewed "revelation" in the central space has symbolic significance for the local community.[21]

After the Communist regime fell in 1989, it became possible again to identify with the history that had been taboo for over half a century. Tomáš and Jan A. Baťa at once became heroes throughout what was again Czechoslovakia. Despite

Figure 5. The choice of the photograph on the cover of the 1964 book *Partizánske v bojoch a budování* [Partizánske in battles and in building] clearly illustrates the Communist regime's attempt to break continuity with the past by not showing any traces of Baťa's architecture. Pavel Kapusta, *Partizánske v bojoch a budování* (Bratislava: Osveta, 1964).

this, Baťa architecture is now in some jeopardy, because unsystematic legislation and unbridled capitalism have given historic preservation institutions little time to develop appropriate strategies (throughout the country's territory). The urban structure completed in the later twentieth century (town hall, cultural center) kept to the intentions of Voženílek's layout, albeit using that period's architectural style and with altered functions, but later interventions have gradually clouded the town's original aesthetic.

3. Reflecting on the Shift in Historic Preservation Discourse

The factory area, with buildings arranged in a grid, still retain their multi-story production halls with facades of characteristic red-brick masonry and exposed reinforced concrete construction, but some new proprietors have "brightened" them with unbecoming paint jobs. Owners of individual houses, in addition to understandably fencing their yards for privacy—contrary to the original concept—have put additions and insulation layers on their homes. Also, the former hotel

"Spoločenský dom" (Community House) has been altered. Exceptionally, two of the town square's original buildings have remained almost untouched—Baťa school dormitories for young women and young men—but in contrast to Zlín they have exterior stucco walls.

The weak level of preserving the original Baťa architecture as well as its dissimilarity to Zlín have blurred the town's identity. Added to the dominating view of cultural/historical heritage promoted by institutionalized discourse, this has resulted in difficulty protecting the existing values. This is largely because this discourse emphasizes the material essence of cultural sites while overlooking the value of intangible cultural heritage. This paradigm is changing only gradually, although many progressive theories endeavor to transform prevailing discourse since already two decades.

In her book *Uses of Heritage* the Heritage and Museum Studies scholar Laurajane Smith argued that all historic sites are *a priori* essentially intangible; this does not imply abandoning their tangible forms, but rather that these forms are not the singular essence of their heritage.[22] The preservationist and urban planner Randall Mason similarly holds that the *fabric-centered* bias of the historic preservation field has created a myth of objectivity, and must be balanced with an approach of *values-centered* theories.[23] This approach as an alternative to traditional thinking oriented on physical substance redirects the emphasis to "memories, ideas, and other social motivations that drive the urge to physically preserve the built environment."[24]

While the understanding that architectural heritage cannot be perceived only through its fabric is still relevant, recent publications move the discourse even further;[25] one influential strand of scholarship promoted among others by the researchers Andrea Jelić and Aleksandar Staničić, focuses on the role of the embodied human experience in the processes of making meaning of heritage.[26] While these ideas build on the discourse of architectural phenomenology, as was already promoted mainly by Christian Norberg-Schulz, Juhani Pallasmaa, Pérez-Gómez, and Dalibor Veselý, they find reinforcement in architectural theory and practice that placed "the experiencing and perceiving human body as a central concern of architectural design," as particularly influenced by the phenomenology of embodiment as presented in Merleau-Ponty's work.[27]

It was not only the above-mentioned theories that led us to shift attention toward people's bodily experiences of Partizánske, but also awareness of the recent field of research of embodied cognition.[28] That is why we grew interested in how discussion within the focus group—presented in the next part—might reveal more than just participants' intellectual knowledge about the value of the town. This is not to say our research has attempted to apply methods of neurophenomenology;[29] in our case the aim was to make possible a change in the current understanding of the problem by figuring out what kind of bodily experience of space is involved in the first place.

4. Focus Group

As already mentioned, we entered Partizánske with an existing understanding, mainly related to our knowledge of Baťa towns and their architectural and urban principles. At the same time, we knew the conditions and reasons for the historic preservation policies applied in Zlín. Since we saw that the painstaking efforts to introduce state historic preservation policies were not successful, we asked ourselves how the city is understood and interpreted by people with the intention of monument protection for Partizánske. This required more than just studying archive sources and analytical texts by current historians (of architecture). Our interest in finding out how people who commonly use the town space experience it reinforced the importance of including a sociological perspective, by means of the *focus group* method. This is qualitative research intended to collect data from group discussions moderated by the researcher, to encourage participants to interact. While this is not a frequent method in phenomenological research, it creates the possibility of opening various topics that are not part of the issues as understood previously. This feature of the approach proved worthwhile. As we will show later, this research event (focus group) certainly opened up a new perspective. We analyzed the data obtained from this research event inductively. We drew on the communications of our communication partners, the focus group participants to create our own interpretation of their vision of the city based on their discussion and insights.

We organized a focus group in December 2022, with eight participants aged roughly 20 to 70, most of them born in or long-term residents of town, or residents of nearby villages, with a shared interest in Partizánske.[30] The majority were members of or have regularly taken part in the activities of several local civic organizations.[31] This was not a group with direct experience with the factory's work, but they knew of it through relatives or acquaintances. This combination was not disadvantageous, as our effort was to identify the town's value aspects that even less-informed visitors could take in.

The questions asked concentrated on Partizánske's central space, as this is shared by much of the diverse population, possesses a mix of functions, and connects to the other zones. It was anticipated that this particular space, with the greatest potential of being formative for the town, might be culminating for perceiving the Partizánske identity; additionally, it has undergone several fundamental changes, as we have mentioned. The first round of questions centered on understanding Partizánske's current identity, and the second sought an answer to how the users experience the town, where they get a positive feeling and where not.

To our surprise, although when describing the town, the participants remarked on the factory's presence and the town's Baťa origin as being fundamental, later the group members did not mention such themes.[32] It is as if the working-class past and experience were set aside as of lesser import. The name "Baťa" itself was present throughout, even characterized paternalistically—as looking after employee well-being—though it later became clear they were thinking not of J. A. Baťa but rather using a proxy term for anyone from local factory management. This image of a benevolent "father" company accompanied a simplified notion that all the town's positive aspects are "from Baťa," and an uncritical characterization of the Baťa company as one interested in "building something for people and not just for itself."[33]

Despite this somewhat distorted view of the past, for the future forming of the town identity it is important to appreciate that the Baťa history is something the local people regard as fundamental. This is reflected in an acknowledgment of the value of many buildings even where they have been unbecomingly altered. Participants noted a need to return to the original aspect—"like in Zlín"—of the mixed-use "Spoločenský dom" in addition to the church. There was in the discussion an interest in at least partially giving back to the town the period look; one such association was that everyone considered the demolition of the mid-rise positively because by opening up the view of the church "the Baťa air" was highlighted.

Discussion included an activity with a printed orthophotomap that covered the central space and adjacent areas. Participants were asked to mark, with colored stickers, specific places based on instructions; our interest was how they experience the space. The focus group—aiming to gather new information on the social reality, rather than to evaluate participants' intellectual awareness—facilitated interesting expressions from participants during the interactive discussion, particularly as discussion grew more spontaneous. The next part of the text focuses on the phenomenon of walking, which was identified as a key aspect in the initial part of the focus group. Instead of the static concept of heritage as something we "come to, see, and move on," our communication partners opened up a much more dynamic perspective on which city value deserves to be protected.

Figure 6. Period photographs showing "walking women" of Partizánske/ Baťovany: mothers with baby strollers walking toward the factory site and young women from the Baťa's "school of work." Courtesy of Department of Architecture, Institute of History of the Slovak Academy of Sciences and Courtesy of Anna Poláková.

5. The Walking Phenomenon

The importance of walking gradually began to emerge during the focus group discussion itself. One of the younger focus group participants, when asked how she would introduce her town to visitors who knew nothing about it, replied that to understand it, one needed to know the basic route through the city. Her answer is certainly influenced by the fact that she organizes guided tours, yet it indicates an important point: without the experience of moving around town on foot, it is impossible to understand the basic idea of its urban planning, "how it still works in the city. I would show the basic route where we see the factory and how it connects to the city, and understand after walking there that the city is practical." It was the link between walking and practicality that was key for focus group participants. If it can be walked, it is practical because it must also mean that all important things are within walking distance. As mentioned by an older participant: "It is a complex city where all functions are concentrated in a relatively small area, where it is not necessary to use a car every day, where one is close to nature and really everything one needs to live [. . .] the value is that we see the uniqueness of that complex, the complex of all the functions in the city." So as with the others, there is reference to the whole, not to individual objects in the town. This reveals an essential feature of the city (and of all other Baťa cities): the visitor does not need to see the important buildings, does not need to move from point to point; the very movement through the city, the experiencing of it, is an essential part of the experience of the city and its genius loci.

Our understanding prior to this research had a static character. Thus, only later did we grasp, because repeated responses about walking in the focus group drew it to our attention, that walking is more than just something determinative for the Partizánske urban plan historically; indeed, it is significant in how its users now experience the town physically through their bodies. Yet not even the Norwegian architect Christian Norberg-Schulz, renowned for taking inspiration from phenomenology, placed sufficient emphasis in his *genius loci* theory on the role played by movement through the

Figure 7. Guided walking tours organized by the local civil society Fabrika umenia (Art Factory), 2019 and 2022. Courtesy of Fabrika umenia and dvaja.

perceived space, as the urban development specialist M. Reza Shirazi has noted[34]—although Shirazi goes on to acknowledge Norberg-Schulz's first book *Intentions in Architecture* mentioning the necessity of perceiving architecture by means of movement, which makes it possible to experience it not in isolation but "as a part of a comprehensive urban organism."[35]

It was not just proximity to the center and the excellent pedestrian accessibility that participants praised. Their very perceptions were repeatedly described by way of pedestrian flow. Mention was made of walking through wind, which was stronger when the now-demolished "tall building" was present.[36] This documents that such memories are not merely visual, but rather recalled as a comprehensive physical experience. They described the park behind the demolished dormitory as "parade-ground-like," stimulating people to move around in it—though this could have negative connotations, as one younger participant commented that one felt the need to get out of it because the dormitory created a barrier beyond which she did not feel safe. Intriguingly, what one participant saw as problematic—that the park is quite exposed and thus provides no privacy—is a typical aspect of Baťa urban planning, as the company took some pains to keep track of its employees.[37] Whereas in Baťa days walking was a necessity for most workers, as opposed to "flaneurism," and a pedestrian town meant providing celebratory parades rather than romantic strolls, today there is a different connotation.

In Partizánske, walking can be above all an effective tool to build identity. Indeed, watching the world around via the dynamic of walking has inspired such writers as Winfried George Sebald and Iain Sinclair to make walking a central motif in their work. The synergy in walking through the town today—in a form like the guided walk by the local civil society Fabrika umenia—can foster people to take ownership of the desired town identity. In the future however it will be necessary for the town's authorities to make possible pedestrian traffic in town to be prioritized, as here too car transportation began to take precedence in the twentieth century. In addition, as in other cities, many functions are being relegated to shopping malls

Figure 8. Spatial relations of the central space consisting of a square (left) and park culminating with the church (right) in the collage by architecture studio PLURAL from a winning proposal created for a 2021 competition call for urban/architectural/land planning proposals for the central space. Plural Architects.

at the outskirts; this concerned the focus group participants, as they realize they are losing their reason to spend time in the center. In spite of this, it can be anticipated that, because "walkability" is characteristic of a town's quality, as the urban designer Jeff Speck is now actively advocating,[38] the return of Partizánske's character—as a pedestrian town—is not unrealistic. The city leadership's interest in keeping the center vibrant is also indicated by a recent competition call for urban/architectural/land planning proposals for the central space (2021) that has brought hope that the town will soon see some positive change, even though it was out of the competition scope to set an overall approach to historical heritage.[39]

Conclusion

The main aim of this text was to reflect, through a transdisciplinary approach, how it would be possible to approach the historic preservation of a small functionalist town such as Partizánske. We believe that the poor condition of Baťa architecture in Partizánske need not preclude the town's shaping a future identity, if there is interest in maintaining links to its history. As we were aware of the failure of previous efforts, we wanted to test changes that current theoretical approaches could potentially bring about by involving the residents themselves through the sociological method of the focus group. Involving them was all the more important because, in addition to how they conceptualize and interpret the town's values, we were interested in what aspects they value in terms of how they use the city itself.

Means exist that, alongside institutionalized historic preservation at the national or municipal level, could increase resident/user interest in conserving the Baťa architectural heritage and original urban concept. Moreover, the most effective historic preservation is that supported by the general public, not forced by legislative measures. An open approach to historic preservation, which does not limit itself to traditional inputs but seeks new interpretations, while also considering user responses, has a greater chance of success. This is what influenced us to go beyond the architectural and historical methods that characterize previous research, as these did not have a significant impact on practice.

The nonstandard qualitative sociological research focus group method, and phenomenology as a starting point, supported by progressive perspectives on historic preservation, enabled us fresh interpretation of the "banal" movement of walking. We ourselves were surprised by how the focus group facilitated our interpretation of a well-known feature of Partizánske's urban plan, and simultaneously confirmed how even small departures from standard perspectives can deepen understanding of a problem. Walking can be taken as not only an intangible value in an original urban plan but also an activity that consciously heightens our physical experience of being-in-the-world and become a financially inexpensive instrument of historic preservation. This all the more so because there is reason to hope that in the future walking in Partizánske will again become a preferred means of transportation, dynamically tying together not just the town's individual zones but the Baťa past as well.

Biographies

Nina Bartošová is an associate professor of architectural theory at the Faculty of Architecture and Design, STU in Bratislava, Slovakia, and at the Faculty of Architecture, Brno University of Technology, Czech Republic. She is a co-author of the publication *Industrial Heritage in the Eyes of Expertise/Experience* (2016), author of number of journal articles on the topic of industrial heritage and its preservation from a more recent theoretical viewpoint. Her research approach builds on the experience acquired from both architectural practice and academic environment in several European cities. Her long-term research focuses on the work of Baťa's architect Vladimír Karfík.

Barbora Vacková is a sociologist at Masaryk University, Brno, Czech Republic. She focuses systematically on the sociology of space, urbanism, architecture, and housing. She is the author of the book *Space, Power, and Utopia: The Ideal City and its Society* (2010), and coeditor of several academic monographs (e.g., *The Third City*, 2012; *Alone at Home*, 2015) and monothematic journal issues. Her specialization is long-term research on Bata's cities. She is the co-author of *Vanishing Elements of Zlín Architecture*, focused on the housing policy of the Bata Shoe Company in Zlín, Czech Republic, and the architectural forms of company residential houses.

Veronika Rypák Vaňo is a PhD candidate at the Institute of History and Theory of Architecture and Monument Preservation at the Faculty of Architecture and Design, STU in Bratislava. Her scholarly research concentrates on the twentieth century, primarily Baťa architecture in Partizánske. In her dissertation work she is exploring conservation of Baťa architecture in Slovakia and abroad and alternative possibilities for its protection. A collaborator in architecture education workshops, she assists in preparing programs on the values of Baťa architecture at public events in Partizánske. She is also active in the practice of architecture.

Notes

[1] This is also suggested by the title of the article "Baťovany—Slovak Zlín," published just after World War II, before the Communist regime took over. Ed. Kopečný, "Baťovany—Slovenský Zlín," *Průmyslový Průkopník*, no. 7 (1946): 7–10.

[2] Several texts have already tackled the issue of the identity of Partizánske, among them: Veronika Vaňová and Jana Pohaničová, "Baťovany—(Re)Visions of a Modern Town: Searching for Identity," *ALFA. Architecture Papers of the Faculty of Architecture and Design STU* 27, no. 2 (2022): 24–34. Alena Kubová-Gauché and Isabelle Gournay, "Baťovany-Partizánske: A Functionalist Company Town in Slovakia," in *Iconic Planned Communities and the Challenge of Change*, ed. Mary Corbin Sies,

Isabelle Gournay, and Robert Freestone (Philadelphia: University of Pennsylvania Press, 2019), 368–72.

[3] For example, Nina Bartošová and Katarína Haberlandová, *Industriál očami odborníkov/pamätníkov. Teória a metodológia ochrany priemyselného dedičstva v kontexte Bratislavy* [Industrial heritage in the eyes of expertise/experience. Theory and methodology of industrial heritage conservation in the context of Bratislava] (Bratislava: Vydavateľstvo STU, 2016); Barbora Vacková, Klára Eliášová and Jitka Ressová, *Baťovský domek: Mizející prvky zlínské architektury* [The Baťa home: Zlín's vanishing architectural elements] (Brno: Masarykova univerzita, 2017).

[4] High profit was ensured by increased productivity even with above-average employee compensation.

[5] The company was founded by the Baťa siblings back in the Austro-Hungarian era in 1904 as a shoemaker's shop, and from 1900 it became a public trading company under the name A. & T. Baťa. Tomáš Baťa did not hesitate—even as a company owner—to get a job as a regular laborer to observe production organization in American companies, together with several of his employees. Vladimír Marko, *Šimonovany-Baťovany (1938–1949)* (Partizánske: Spolu sme Slovensko, 2015), 29–30.

[6] It is assumed that the module created the company's construction department by conversion from imperial units based on knowledge of the maximum load capacity of the Reinforced Concrete Structure. More in Ladislava Horňáková, "Construction Department of the Baťa Company: Builder Arnošt Sehnal and the Issue of Anonymity of Company Architects and Builders," in *The Architecture and Urban Planning of the Baťa Concern as One of the Modernisation Factors in Slovakia*, Symposium proceedings, October 21, 2015, Partizánske, ed. Klára Kubičková (Banská Bystrica: C.A.L.E.H. n.o., 2016), 94–101.

[7] A comprehensive description of the Baťa system is described by Zachary Austin Doleshal, *In the Kingdom of Shoes: Bata, Zlin, Globalization, 1894–1945* (Toronto: University of Toronto Press, 2021).

[8] Pavel Novák, *Zlínska Architektura 1900–1950 (1)*, 2. rošír. vyd. (Zlín: POZIMOS, a.s., 2008), 269.

[9] For the first time in the early 1990s, the Monuments Board in nearby Topoľčany developed a concept for the preservation of the original Baťa part of the town, including specific important buildings. However, no agreement between the Monuments Board and the town representatives was made. See Henrieta Moravčíková, "Baťovany-Partizánske: Vzorné priemyselné mesto na Slovensku. Baťovany—Partizánske: An exemplary industrial city in Slovakia," *Architektúra & Urbanizmus* 37, nos. 3–4 (2003): 141.

[10] At the same time, the company also bought and expanded a tannery in Nové Zámky, in Lower Nitra, and in the 1930s it started production in Svit, in the Low Tatras basin. See Henrieta Moravčíková, "Baťovany-Partizánske," 114.

[11] Ted Shelton, "Automobile Utopias and Traditional Urban Infrastructure: Visions of the Coming Conflict, 1925–1940," *Traditional Dwellings and Settlements Review* 22, no. 2 (2011): 64.

[12] Kubová-Gauché and Gournay, "Baťovany-Partizánske," 368. Also in Alena Kubová, "Znovuobjavenie Funkčného Mesta," in *Partizánske: Réinventer La Ville Fonctionnelle. Znovuobjavenie Funkčného Mesta*, ed. Katalóg Výstavy, Alena Kubová (Bratislava: Vydavateľstvo Spolku architektov Slovenska, 2005), 7. See also Juraj Janto, "Moderné Mesto a Jeho Kultúrne Dedičstvo—Príklad Partizánskeho a Novej Dubnice. Modern City and Its Cultural Heritage—The Example of Partizánske and Nová Dubnica," *Muzeológia a Kultúrne Dedičstvo* 7, no. 2 (2019): 112.

[13] Originally the railway line crossed the promenade; in 1975 an underpass was built in the given place as a safer solution, but the visual connection of the factory with the city was weakened.

[14] Peter Andráši, "Zrod Prvého Moderného Mesta Na Slovensku. Urbanistický Vývoj Partizánskeho v Jeho Počiatočnom Období (ca 1938–1960)," *Monument Revue* 2 (2013): 23.

[15] From 1 January 1939, this company became the owner of all businesses in Slovakia, including three hundred stores. Pavel Kapusta, *Partizánske v Bojoch a Budovaní* (Bratislava: Osveta, 1964), 45.

[16] This could have been an intentional change in the company's strategy. See Nina Bartošová, "Karfík's 'Swedish' Balconies: The Shift from the Garden City Conception to Scandinavian Inspiration in the Context of Baťa Company Housing in Zlín," *Architektúra & Urbanizmus* 56, nos. 3–4 (2022): 213.

[17] Mária Topolčanská and Slávka Doricová, "Variácie Štandardu Individuálneho Bývania Firmy Baťa / Variations of Individual Housing Standard of the Baťa Company," *Architektúra & Urbanizmus* 47, nos. 3–4 (2003): 159.

[18] Henrieta Moravčíková, "Problematic Heritage: Architecture and Urban Planning of the Baťa Concern in Slovakia," in *The Architecture and Urban Planning of the Baťa Concern as One of the Modernisation Factors in Slovakia*, ed. Kubičková, 26.

[19] This has been noted in Nina Bartošová, "Kontext Priestoru a Času: Kostol v Baťovanoch-Partizánskom," in *Architektura v Perspektivě 2020. Ostrava, 14.–15. 10, 2020*, ed. Martina Peřinková (Ostrava: VŠB—Technická univerzita Ostrava, 2020), 10–15. The church's construction took place from 1943 to 1949 and it was listed as a National Cultural Monument in 1996. Monuments Board of the Slovak Republic, "Register pamiatkových objektov," 15 January 2023, https://www.pamiatky.sk/nkp-a-po/register-po/objekt-detail/?idObjekt=4545.

[20] Tomáš Baťa allegedly said that "politics and religion are not for sale, therefore we have nothing to do with them either." As in Marko, *Šimonovany-Baťovany (1938–1949)*, 31.

[21] The church as a community symbol is mentioned by Alena Kubová, ed., *Partizánske: Réinventer La Ville Fonctionnelle. Znovuobjavenie Funkčného Mesta. Katalóg Výstavy* (Bratislava: Vydavateľstvo Spolku architektov Slovenska, 2005), 8.

[22] Laurajane Smith, *Uses of Heritage*, 1st ed. (London: Routledge, 2006), 3.

[23] Randall Mason, "Fixing Historic Preservation: A Constructive Critique of 'Significance,'"*Places* 16, no. 1 (2004): 67–68.

[24] Mason, "Fixing Historic Preservation, 68.

[25] Including a recent book by Laurajane Smith, *Emotional Heritage. Visitor Engagement at Museums and Heritage Sites* (London: Routledge, 2021) that interprets heritage as a "process, practice or performative activity."

[26] Andrea Jelić and Aleksandar Staničić, "Embodiment and Meaningmaking: Interdisciplinary Perspectives on Heritage Architecture," *The Journal of Architecture* 27, no. 4 (2022): 473–84.

[27] Andrea Jelić and Aleksandar Staničić, "The Memory in Bodily and Architectural Making," in *Reflections from Embodied Cognitive Science Affective Architectures: More-Than-Representational Geographies of Heritage*, ed. Jacque Micieli-Voutsinas and Angela M. Person (London: Taylor & Francis Group, 2020), 187.

[28] As pursued by Shaun Gallagher, Thomas Fuchs: Thomas Fuchs, "Collective Body Memories," in *Embodiment, Enaction, and Culture: Investigating the Constitution of the Shared World*, ed. Christoph Durt, Thomas Fuchs, and Christian Tewes (Cambridge, MA: The MIT Press, 2017); Shaun Gallagher, *How the Body Shapes the Mind* (Oxford: Clarendon Press, 2005).

[29] See in Andrea Jelić, "Designing "Pre-reflective" Architecture: Implications of Neurophenomenology for Architectural Design and Thinking," *Ambiances* [online], no. 1 (2015), https://journals.openedition.org/ambiances/628.

[30] This was presumably one reason why they gave us an hour and a half of their time and agreed to an audio recording of the meeting.

[31] The local civil society Fabrika umenia helped organize the focus group for the purposes of our research.

[32] The purpose of the second round of questions was to find out how participants characterized the city, what they imagined when they heard the name of Baťa, and what they specifically considered necessary to preserve.

[33] A female native from Partizánske (age 50) during the focus group in the Baťa Info point (Partizánske, December 18, 2022). More on the inclusion of non-Baťa historical contexts, see Barbora Vacková and Nina Bartošová, "Baťovany—Partizánske: Contemporary Re/inventing the Heritage of the Baťa Company Town," *Český lid/ Czech Ethnological Journal 111*, no. 2 (2024): 199–219.

[34] M. Reza Shirazi, *Towards an Articulated Phenomenological Interpretation of Architecture: Phenomenal Phenomenology* (London: Routledge, 2013), 63

[35] Christian Norberg-Schulz, *Intentions in Architecture* (Cambridge, MA: The MIT Press, 1965), 198.

[36] The building disturbed the air flow encouraged by the original master plan, which was supposed to cool the residential zones around the square, as mentioned by one of the participants.

[37] Barbora Vacková, "Organizované Město" (The Organized City), in *Baťovský domek: mizející prvky zlínské architektury (The Baťa Home: Zlín's Vanishing Architectural Elements)*, ed. Barbora Vacková, Klára Eliášová, and Jitka Ressová (Brno: Masarykova univerzita, 2017), 19–33, in English, 234–41.

[38] Jeff Speck, *WALKABLE CITY: How Downtown Can Save America, One Step at a Time*, Reprint edition (New York: North Point Press, 2013). Note: Both the importance of everyday walking and the connection to phenomenological perspective is specifically discussed in Stine Rybråten, Margrete Skår, and Helena Nordh, "The Phenomenon of Walking: Diverse and Dynamic," *Landscape Research* 44, no. 1 (2 January 2019): 62–74.

[39] The architectural studio PLURAL took first place. Archinfo, "Obnova Námestia SNP a Parku J. A. Baťu v Partizánskom—výsledky súťaže," June 11, 2021, https://www.archinfo.sk/diela/obnova-namestia-snp-a-parku-j-a-batu-v-partizanskom-vysledky-sutaze.html.

Figure 1. Wong arrives at the Ko Shan Theatre stop in the film's opening. Screenshot: Frame 1 of "When in Doubt, Take a Walk" (2020). Copyright © Sampson Wong.

Sony Devabhaktuni

Walking as Infrastructural Practice

Provisioning in Sampson Wong's "When in Doubt"

Introduction

The heritage of political dissent in Hong Kong was rewritten with social unrest that began in the spring of 2019. Actions dispersed throughout the territory and restrictions on movement and gathering that followed transformed daily life. COVID-19's global spread in early 2020 offered additional justification for these restrictions. In the summer of that year, the Communist Party of China imposed a National Security Law (NSL) with ambiguous red lines that blurred what freedoms existed in Hong Kong: in January 2021, the detention of forty-seven progressive opposition leaders darkened the city's mood and further occluded the events of 2019, making the revindication for another future a distant possibility. Those months had a visceral impact on Hong Kong and its people: attachments to each other and to affectively charged events marked identities and imaginations. Nevertheless, Hong Kong's leaders, motivated in part by the edicts of the NSL, have worked to efface traces of unrest and forbid its memorialization. For some in Hong Kong, one question that lingers is how to remember those events within an official context that demands forgetting. As with the government's more recent interdiction of commemorations of the 1989 protests at Tiananmen Square, the executive's legitimacy increasingly depends on cutting links to a practice of dissent that had earlier been inscribed into the city's material and social fabric. In light of an enforced proscription on recollecting, how is it then possible to pass down this heritage of contestation? And through that transmission, how can remembrance not be an artifact of extinguished possibility, but rather an active and felt potential within the present into future?

This article considers a practice that offers a response to these questions. Sampson Wong's "When in Doubt, Take a Walk" ["When in Doubt"] is a YouTube series and channel that documents solitary outings through Hong Kong's neighborhoods.[1] Each of the roughly five-minute videos that began the project—made with videographer Eric Tsang—follows Wong or another solitary protagonist through a different district: its parks, housing projects, esplanades, walkways, stairs, and streets. Along with ambient sounds of the city, the early videos have soundtracks composed by Joshua Chiu. A closing request to like and share offers viewers the chance to support a Patreon channel where it is also possible to find a written

Future Anterior
Volume XX, Numbers 1–2
Summer / Winter 2023

description of the itinerary. These directions begin from local landmarks and shops, meaning they are best pursued when one physically goes to the point of departure. The channel now includes dozens of short videos including walks made independently—by friends or strangers—some following the model of the earliest films.

Where earlier artistic and urban practices offer ways to think about how walking articulates relations between the city, movement, and memory, those precedents are unable to account for the collective nature of Wong's mediated practice or what I propose is a specifically infrastructural orientation toward the city. My understanding of infrastructure follows Lauren Berlant's redefinition of the term in relation to structure and social transformation. I consider Wong's work through a task that Berlant identifies for makers of critical social form in times of breakdown when an important role is to offer possibilities for making it through a difficult meanwhile. For Berlant, this infrastructuring allows for the distribution of resources, maintenance, and care. As a provisioning, infrastructure as a form of life requires a rethinking of the commons that it sustains, so that as a concept, the commons remains open to the ambivalence, tension, and disagreement that underlies any shared realm. With Berlant's guidance, I'd like to consider Wong's practice as one in which the memory of difficult attachments is guarded and maintained as an ambivalent common. It is this very ambivalence, and the space it opens for disagreement, that Hong Kong's increasingly enforced regime of stability and right-thinking seeks to annul from public life, making any recollection of that heritage of contestation itself proscribed.[2]

The Anti-ELAB Protests of 2019–2020

Protests that began in 2019 and spread into 2020 against a proposed extradition bill [Anti-ELAB protests] differed from movements earlier in the decade.[3] These earlier protests were localized in both real space and in symbolic force while the anti-ELAB protests took place all over the city. Marches, actions and events in multiple places at multiple times of day and night resulted in an all-overness to the trauma of conflict, investing sites throughout the city with longing and brutality.[4]

The public's engagement with these events changed the city's landscape. Protest actions involved the removal of streetside barriers, the taking apart of sidewalks or the dismantling of elevators and escalators. Other physical changes to the city took the form of graffiti and poster-campaigns; "Lennon Walls" comprising hundreds of Post-it notes, flowers, and objects lined the walls of metro stations and offered people an opportunity to react to the events.[5] These ubiquitous acts transformed daily life in ways imbued with affective force: anger, empathy, sadness, and the anxious uncertainty of what would come next.

These traces of protests were quickly removed or repaired, while any commemoration of the events was circumscribed by an official language of condemnation. "Lennon Walls" were dismantled, graffiti painted over, and street side barriers replaced and reinforced with new security bolts that prevent their easy taking apart. While the government has more recently spoken of the period as one of "black violence" and vaunted a return to "stability," the weight and significance of the period remains an important heritage of the city's recent past.

Crackdown also coincided with a time when COVID-19 made being together and moving through parts of the city difficult. Playgrounds, picnic areas, and athletic facilities were closed, while gatherings were ostensibly limited. Mandatory hotel quarantine periods stretching to twenty-one days at the height of restrictions effectively closed off the city from the world. That those restrictions were often convoluted into the earlier, protest-related measures of control, meant that many of spaces of daily life were charged with restriction. What freedoms Hong Kong had before 2019 were effectively stifled through a reasoning that wove together logics of health and security into an inscrutable and ambiguous illegality.

Wong has spoken about the intense sense of hopelessness that came over many friends during these events—the securitization of the city seeming to have foreclosed action or empathetic relations with their home.[6] Doubt about what to do and how to continue in the face of intense ambivalence pervaded. Wong points, for example, to a banner displayed during one of the city's last mass marches. Stretching many meters and held in place by many hands, it could be translated as "We really fucking love Hong Kong," reflecting the anger, belonging, and frustration that come together to explain a seemingly unshakeable insistence on staying.[7]

"When in Doubt, Take a Walk"

It is in this context and the very limited scope of operation left open by the government's ambiguous prohibitions that Wong began the YouTube series and channel.[8] Wong's first video was released on October 9, 2020, several months after Hong Kong's first summer of COVID restrictions and a little more than three months after the promulgation of the National Security Law. I first describe the structure of this video before turning to ways of thinking about walking and, with Berlant's help, infrastructure and the commons. I then return to the video to consider how an infrastructural analysis makes the transmission of a heritage of contestation legible.

Figure 2. A second view of an ascent of the stairs to the hilltop reservoir. Screenshot: Frame 33 of "When in Doubt, Take a Walk" (2020). Copyright © Sampson Wong.

Wong's video consists of a sequence of forty-nine still-frame shots together lasting a little more than five minutes; some frames are on the screen for no more than 2 seconds, while several last more than 10 and up to 15. The syncopated editing of images contrasts with a melodic and melancholic piano score. In the opening scene, a local "green bus," parked at the Ko Shan Theater is framed with a park behind it; a sign indicates the stop's name (Figure 1). A man walks to the right of the bus, perhaps having just arrived. It is Wong himself, dressed in a red T-shirt and carrying a cloth satchel over his shoulder, a hand clutching the strap. Wong, like all the people we encounter in the film, is wearing a surgical mask. In the second frame, he appears in the same position on the screen as if his trajectory has continued from the sidewalk directly onto the slope of a ramp that ascends the terrain of a park.

This implication of continuous displacement is one of a number of ways movement coordinates with space and time in the film. Some shots last only so long as Wong's crossing from left to right, or the distance walked toward or into the frame. In some pairings of scenes, time is rewound or repeated: for example, in one shot Wong is climbing a stone stair attached to a retaining wall. A few frames later, Wong appears in the distance ascending those same stairs as if we slip back in time for another perspective of his trajectory (Figure 2). In another pairing, Wong looks toward an elevated walkway that crosses the road directly into a building; three shots later, the framing is repeated, except now Wong makes his way across the bridge (Figures 3 and 4). In one of the video's final scenes, a cross visible through green, fencing mesh was glimpsed earlier at the top of a church. Framed views of the sky, of a cat perched on the slope of a hillside, or of people going about the business

Figure 3. Wong approaching a walkway leading into the housing estate. Screenshot: Frame 16 of "When in Doubt, Take a Walk" (2020). Copyright © Sampson Wong.

Figure 4. A second view, several frames later of Wong crossing the walkway. Screenshot: Frame 19 of "When in Doubt, Take a Walk" (2020). Copyright © Sampson Wong.

of the day are interspersed with Wong's trajectory through the video's sites.

In only one instance does Wong's body come to rest. In a sequence of three frames, Wong first reaches through bars surrounding a vending machine to purchase a drink with his Octopus Card—a digital wallet managed by the city's transport authority. A close-up follows with him sitting on a bench taking a sip of the purchased drink. Wash towels hang to dry on a chain-link fence that encloses tennis courts behind him; a final, wider shot reveals that he is in a play area, recycling bins nearby (Figure 5). A daughter chases after her father as

Figure 5. Wong takes a rest on the hill-top leisure area surrounded by infrastructure. Screenshot: Frame 46 of "When in Doubt, Take a Walk" (2020). Copyright © Sampson Wong.

Wong watches. These frames act as a caesura in the otherwise continuous movement that characterizes the video; in this moment, we take a break in the late afternoon shade and feel the cold of the drink registering the physical effort of walking under the heat and up the site's hilly terrain.

The looping, slipping, and cutting of time and space distinguishes the film from familiar models of urban YouTube videos that, for example, follow a transit route through the city from the front seat of a double decker bus. This spatio-temporal play also prevents the films from being a guided tour along a clearly discernible trajectory. The editorial choices eschew a passive movement through space in favor of an author's close attention.

The video stitches together a route between three adjacent sites. The "Pick-up & Drop-off" for "Ko Shan Theatre Only" in the opening frame identifies a starting point that makes it possible to follow along using "Google Street View." The first part of the film tracks Wong through Ko Shan Park past two buildings that comprise a theater complex: one with a swooping concrete roof and another finished in vertical wooden brise soleil hung along the curve of the façade. Wong winds through the park past two children and their minder, a solitary woman exercising at the side of the path, and a small group of children playing on the vast grounds of an empty concrete sports pitch adjacent to the theater.

In the video's second section, Wong continues into To Kwa Wan, a district immediately north of the park and theatre complex. This second site comprises two housing developments, straddled on one side by an elevated road, and the other by a steeply rising hillside cut away to make room for the towers. The older of the two developments comprise an island of low-rise, five story buildings. Wong walks past these squat blocks toward the second residential estate: towering slabs with similar color schemes, connected by overpasses and terrasses. Winding through slots of space, open air entrance lobbies, and an outdoor common area with condemned concrete ping-pong tables, Wong makes his way up and through the estate.

At its edge, he finds the stairs mentioned earlier. They lead to a path ascending the adjacent hillside. After a climb that takes him past additional small groups and solitary visitors, he arrives at the recreational area that sits atop the engineered ground of a reservoir overlooking Kowloon. Along the way, we see more condemned sports equipment: basketball hoops taped up and outdoor exercise machines tied into place. The film ends shortly after Wong's pause for a drink. In the closing frame, his back is to us as he descends a narrow flight of slope maintenance stairs; each step is painted yellow at the run's edge, and a railing to one side guards against the descending hillside.

As the screen fades into the shadows of the forest, the music continues and a text appears inviting viewers to "like & share" the video and subscribe to the channel. What sense we have of discovery and exploration in the minutes that have passed is qualified by the fleeting nature of those moments and the visceral expenditure of effort that such a walk would entail. At the same time, it is difficult to name or situate what exactly has transpired: what is Wong's specific intention with the video? While there are qualities of feeling that pervade, what exactly is the point?

Walking, City and Subject

Modernist encounters with walking sometimes cast the practice as a mechanism for resituating the subject in relation to the urban realm: the *flaneur*'s scopic relationship to the street and its slowing of time; the *dérive*'s defamiliarization of the urban through the juxtaposition of routes; or Michel de Certeau's assertion that walking "multiplies and concentrates the city itself," shaping "what ought to be."[9] These discourses recognize that movement works in a reciprocal relation to the urban: at once constructing the subject and making the city. In more recent, contemporary walking practices, this relation between subject and city has been stripped of any universalizing articulation. Instead, walking operates through the specificity of a singular engagement.

For example, the scholar Injeong Yoon-Ramirez describes walking as a "sensate experience" that makes possible a "recollective engagement with our memories" opening new forms of knowing.[10] She proposes that "walking-sensing" is a means to "re-engage with the dis-remembered colonial past and resurge the different ways of being and sensing that are suppressed by coloniality."[11] Walking-sensing involves attending to social encounters, people, objects, and places around us and is an invitation to reflect on how and why we sense in the way we do. This relationship between knowledge and memory also makes walking a powerful vector for articulating and inscribing the heritage of a city. The artist Ernest Pujol's practice of walking has been described as a method for "political regeneration" or as "reparative behavior" that functions as a cathartic engagement with a larger societal brokenness: not a solution but a way to open a space within that break-down.[12] David Pinder, writing on Francis Alÿs's walks through Mexico City argues for their "openness and ambivalence" as a method that sets aside notions of "creative resistance, nomadism, and subversion" in favor of walking's "low visibility" "emphasis on passing through" and its "air of clandestine wastefulness, of futile expenditure."[13] These examples resonate in different ways with Wong's practice. They speak to the way it moves away from the crafting of subjectivity in relation to the city, toward more inchoate goals.

Indeed, Wong, his friends, or strangers that take part in the "When in Doubt" series are resolutely themselves, not stand-ins for an every-person; at the same time, their trajectories are proposals for a re-enactment, offerings that incite. In Wong's invitation to "like & share" and to take a walk oneself, there is a prompt to engage in a collective undertaking that contributes to a loosely formed relation to the city. At the same time, the post-NSL, post-COVID context speaks to the walk's reparative and generative quality: this quality is less a transgressive incitation than an invitation to take part in an unannounced passing through. The collective nature of the work suggests that what is at stake is not so much subjectivity and the individual's autonomy to remake themselves and the urban realm, but rather something that exists *between* as a shared, if distinct, experience.

What these contemporary examples also have in common with Wong is the role that documentary images play in their transmission. Such transmission is not entirely new, with written accounts of urban walks playing an important role in recording the past of cities. Franz Hessel's walks through Berlin before World War II are testaments to its lost materiality while also offering a sensible relation to moving through city fabric.[14] The poet Lisa Robertson also notably documented Vancouver's transformation by the flattening and homogenizing forces of finance-driven development at the turn of the twenty-first century. In "Seven Walks," she writes as a "we" alluding to the shared community of "fellow walkers" that were part of the experience of encountering Vancouver.[15] This social nature transforms walking into an intersubjective encounter, in which the city affords affective as well as material and spatial relations.

For Wong, the intersubjective "we" operates through the sharing of the videos themselves and in the way the channel collects and disseminates recordings by others documenting their own trajectories. Wong's peregrinations are mediated events, shared across time and space through the internet. Hessel and Robertson's documentation of the cities they cared for also became an important mechanism for the transmission of heritage. The articulation of routes through the city, acting as an invitation to identify familiar landmarks and trajectories, acts as a gauge of transformation. Wong's videos may someday also act as records of a physically transformed city; but for the moment it would seem that the heritage that his videos attempt to maintain is a close collective experience of more recent traumas.

This history of the Anti-ELAB protests becomes an ambivalent heritage that is not resolved through walking, but rather reaffirmed in its dispersion through—and implication in—the spaces of the city themselves. Everywhere one turns is a memory of an event related to contestation. This ambivalence returns to the origins of the word heritage itself, which, in the Latin *heres,* calls to mind the contemporary words "heir" and "heiress" tying heritage to a person. And in that person, there enters also a notion of loss and bereavement, the status of the heiress activated only with the death of another. The etymology takes us back to a proto root "**ǵʰeh*" that means to come, to reach, to go, to walk, but most relevantly "to abandon." The Ancient Greek *khḗra* that also derives from this root is "widow." On the one hand, therefore, we have a notion of heritage as a positive bringing forward—of lands, property, things—that allows for the maintenance of the past into the present, and on the other we have a notion of abandonment and loss, of walking away. In my mind, these two senses of the word and its origins describes an ambivalent and almost contradictory pull. What is brought into the present as a kind of "gift" to be maintained is also woven through with a pathos of destitution. We become heirs to worlds, places, and things that have been the sites of others whose lives remain lost to us. In walking, "When in Doubt," seeks to maintain a fragile heritage of social and political upheaval in Hong Kong's history as a place, city, and home.

Berlant, Infrastructures and Social Transformation

What is perhaps difficult to recognize in "When in Doubt," is the way it addresses that upheaval. The solitary masked figures and the taped-up playgrounds recall COVID's grip over the city, but otherwise, there is little hint of political protest and no overt recollection of events of that very recent past. If we consider "When in Doubt" through either modernist or contemporary frameworks, those ways of thinking about walking and the city would seem mostly inadequate to supporting a claim for the video's relation to a heritage of contestation. At the same time, we could ask what kind of remembering is even possible in light of ambiguous government prohibitions on political dissent and commemoration? How can a walk through the city transmit this difficult heritage, when hope itself seems to have been extinguished? It is here that I want to turn to Lauren Berlant's rearticulation of infrastructure and the commons to propose that we can better attend to Wong's practice through these redefined concepts.

Lauren Berlant's questioning of the "kind of form of life an infrastructure is" acts as an interrogation of the meanings we ascribe to infrastructure, the ways it functions to sustain and organize our lives, and its role in social transformation.[16] This interrogation continues a line of thought that resonates with the sociologist Susan Leigh Star's study of infrastructural breakdown.[17] Starr argued that we become aware of the networks that allow for the movement of life-sustaining resources only in that moment when they cease to function: the hand that turns the faucet to let loose a sputtering immediately calls forth not only a network of pipes, tunnels, and reservoirs in that instant of failure but also the people tasked with maintaining and repairing such systems.

This opening toward the human infrastructures that undergird the functioning of a material emplacement reorients infrastructure toward those people that maintain life-sustaining resources. From these human networks of material maintenance, we could also shift our thinking toward those charged with caring for others, bringing us to a capacious "form of life" that extends from the highway to the nurse-practitioner. Starr's identification of breakdown as important to the revelation of the people that maintain physical infrastructural emplacements, speaks as well to Berlant's own desire to understand the role of infrastructure as a form of life in those moments of social disruption that themselves break down lives, families, and communities.

Breakdown also foregrounds infrastructure's affective role. The workings of systems—whether material or human networks—have an emotional charge that calls forth various forms of attachment. Brian Larkin describes the "promise" and "poetry" of infrastructure that imbues highways, irrigation systems, airports, and radio broadcasts at different scales of subject- and nation-building.[18] We could equally speak of the way other forms of infrastructural life have their own affective charge: becoming the sites of gratitude, awe, and anger, while simultaneously, in other instances, going unremarked in their sustaining roles as agents of differential distributions.

Important to Berlant's questioning of infrastructure is the way they define it in relation to structure, and the way the latter itself is redefined. Berlant proposes that "an infrastructural analysis helps us see that what we commonly call 'structure' is not what we usually call it, an intractable principal of continuity across time and space, but is really a convergence of force and value in patterns of movement that's only solid when seen from a distance."[19] The seeming fixity of structure then is not pre-given and permanent but rather a momentary configuration of distributions that reflects the dominance of certain values at any given instant. To get away from this notion of stability or hardness, Berlant proposes a "redefining of 'structure'" as "*that which organizes transformation*"; as such, structure is recast not as fixity but as a for-some-time configuration that ultimately is also what articulates change.[20] Berlant continues by "redefining . . . 'infrastructure' as that which binds us to the world in movement and keeps the world practically bound to itself."[21] If structure is the organization of transformation, a seeming fixity that has within it the potential for remaking, then infrastructure in Berlant's redefinition would be those straps, attachments, and links that sustain us through the difficulty of structure's transformation. In those times when the hardness of structure seems to be undergoing a dissolution, it is infrastructure that makes it possible to hold on. That *making possible* is both a sustaining through that transition and a resourcing that helps to shape it. As "the living mediation of what organizes life: the lifeworld of structure"—infrastructure then is an articulatory fluid that at once aliments and nourishes structure's provisional articulation while also offering the potential to loosen what appears stable.[22] This potential is dependent on infrastructure's viscosity and the speeds at which it courses between those seemingly fixed elements. This way of thinking challenges the stability and closed object-ness of the world.

In this redefining of infrastructure and structure, Berlant identifies a role for those who seek to negotiate this imbricated relation. They propose that "one task for makers of critical social form is to offer not just judgment about positions and practices in the world, but terms of transition that alter the harder and softer, tighter and looser infrastructures of sociality itself."[23] These "terms of transition" are experiments for a broken world that make it possible to "forge an imaginary for managing the meanwhile within damaged life's perdurance" that simultaneously "allows for ambivalence, distraction, antagonism and inattention not to destroy collective existence."[24] What Berlant is proposing then are strategies for encounter that become propositions for the viscosity that binds structures together: these are experiments that forestall the destruction of collective life despite enduring damage, but also potentially allow for the unloosening of structure to allow for transformational social change. That Berlant proposes that makers of critical form offer "not just judgement about positions and practices" speaks to the role such offerings can play even while suspending an overt critique.[25] Indeed, "managing the meanwhile" can be about making space for the contradictory and conflicting sets of relations that characterize strife, and the need to continue living through such moments of "damaged life's perdurance."

Within the idea of a "world practically bound to itself" Berlant also takes care to specify that what they are speaking about is not a "commons" in which difference, ambivalence, and contestation are flattened within a notion of the good, the same, or the ideal. They argue against the "prestige of the commons concept . . . as an ontology that merely needs the world to create infrastructures to catch up to it."[26] Such a reduction evades the necessarily agonistic nature of any shared realm and the work, negotiation, and conflict that underlies its articulation as an in-between; infrastructure plays a role not after such a process is complete—"to catch up to it"—but operates within that very process itself, as part of the settlements that allow for difference to take form. Too often, for Berlant, when we speak about the commons it is "a way of talking about politics as the resolution of ambivalence and the vanquishing of the very contingency of nonsovereign standing."[27] This nonsovereignty is a relational dependence that rejects atomization while at the same time recognizing difference. Nonsovereign standing is the simultaneous and reciprocal understanding of interdependence and independence, an acknowledgement of mutual need in the face of difference. Sociality, as the many or the multiple, is not, in this sense, an agreement upon the same, but rather the negotiation of that distance.

Rather than holding the commons up as an ideal in which strife is extinguished and all values shared, Berlant proposes that a better use for the concept is to "point to a way to view what's broken in sociality," and as an acknowledgment of "the difficulty of convening a world conjointly, although it is inconvenient and hard."[28] In this reframing, the commons is no longer an idealized condition of shared belonging, but rather becomes an object that gauges the inequities that configure the social and acts as a reminder of the difficulties comprising this perpetual undertaking. Similarly, Berlant proposes that the commons as a concept can "offer incitements to imagining a livable provisional life" that become possibilities for "learning to live with messed up yet shared and ongoing infrastructures of experience."[29] The commons thus offers makers of critical social form an incitation to articulate those possibilities for making it through a contemporary brokenness that are rooted in a more complex understanding of that in-between: one in which nonsovereign standing, the agonism of a being together and the affective ambivalences of that collective life, comprise a relation to the world. The provisions that makers of critical social form are able to offer thus do not claim to restore or renew sociality, but instead make it possible to hold together and perdure.

Wong's Infrastructural Practice

My proposal then is that Wong's practice offers "terms of transition" for the specific "meanwhile" that characterizes this moment in Hong Kong's history when a relation to the city is charged with a deeply felt ambivalence. His is an infrastructural practice in the way it aliments distributions—of memory, a care for the city, a relational in-between—that comprise a form of life coursing through the hardness of a changed city in ways that allow for the fixity of this structural configuration to be recognized as semblance.

There are perhaps traces in my earlier description of the video of this reading of infrastructural practice: the mediated nature of Wong's work and the diffusion and replication of the films on YouTube put the city into relation with a dispersed network of people who care for Hong Kong. No guide offers their understanding; instead, the filmic language proposes multiple ways of registering what we see. Cuts in the video between sites eschew a perfect continuity so that walking itself is privileged over viewing. The films propose links without flattening experience into a smooth continuity, impelling a more active investigation. That the videos resist overt positioning or critique to instead foreground an attention to the city and the incitation to reenact such forms of care, speaks to Berlant's proposition that makers of critical social form can sometimes fulfill an important task by offering a certain remove that identifies spaces for ambivalence and uncertainty in times of distress: when that space itself can offer refuge. The films provision for Hong Kong's ongoing "meanwhile"; they aliment and circulate links between places and people awaiting a time when that viscosity allows for a reorganization of what appears in the current moment to be unmovable.

Another look at the first video in Wong's series with Berlant more precisely at hand makes it possible to reconsider the film's choices. In my mind, these choices operate specifically on a particular political moment in Hong Kong when it would seem critical to find some way to situate the events of the Anti-ELAB protests as a heritage to be gathered and brought forward. At the same time, it is the latent quality of the protests, their place in the background, that allows the work to create a space for both remembering and moving on. The title of the series itself "When in doubt, take a walk" refers to the difficulty of this charge. "Taking a walk" in Cantonese has the additional connotation of going to a protest, and this double meaning underlies the films. On Wong's YouTube channel, this original title was later changed, to "When in doubt, just go" suggesting a transformed margin of possibility, a heightened awareness of proscriptions on language, or perhaps a desire to broaden the agenda of the channel to a larger set of engagements with the city's space and people.

Returning to the first video—its starting point at the Ko Shan Park and theater complex, to To Kwa Wan and its collective and social housing blocks, and finally the hill-top recreation complex—an infrastructural analysis immediately puts into focus the way Wong's work articulates different types of material and social infrastructures that sustain the life of the city. Each of the three sites offers a more complex understanding of the role of this infrastructural form of life within contemporary Hong Kong.

The two, government-run theatres in Ko Shan Park reflect, in their architectural styles and missions, a transformed set of values for what comprises public culture in the city. The swooping curved roof of the older theater once fronted an open-air amphitheater that has been transformed in successive iterations into an interior auditorium. The new theater is home to Chinese Opera and comprises an enclosed world largely cut off from the outside. Ko Shan Park, which like the theaters, is managed by the Leisure and Cultural Services Department, comprises a standard Hong Kong model for how "leisure" and "culture" are articulated by government authority and speaks as well to the role that this authority has in nearly all realms of social and public life. The people we encounter in the nearly empty complex—the exercising woman swinging her arms to slap her shoulders, the children and their minder, and the boys playing on the concrete soccer pitch—demonstrate how these spaces are crucial even in those times of restriction when gathering itself is proscribed (Figure 6). The government's role in their management and the decision during COVID to put them off limits, speaks to the ambivalent relation that such a configuration of authority produces.

In the second section of the video, the two housing projects that define the To Kwa Wan district are important examples of alternative models for residential development in Hong Kong. The island of low-rise units that Wong walks by have, after years of resistance, been condemned and sold to a consortium for redevelopment into private flats.[30] The existing units were built in 1953 as part of the Civil Servants' Co-operative Building Society Scheme and remained until the 1970s as a form of housing

Figure 6. A lone woman exercising in Ko Shan Park. Screenshot: Frame 8 of "When in Doubt, Take a Walk" (2020). Copyright © Sampson Wong.

subsidy for Chinese civil servants; the scheme represents a model of collective financing and development that is deemed to be no longer viable despite research concluding that "from a housing environment or neighborhood planning perspective, a co-op should be acclaimed for being the most successful housing policy in Hong Kong."[31] That these low-rise blocks and their large units contribute significant qualities to the neighborhood has not been deemed of value by authorities. Residents were bought out by the government and their community dispersed throughout the city. Infrastructure here as a form of life, can be understood as both this community and the residential blocks that allowed for its articulation over decades. What support the Co-operative Building Society Scheme was able to provide residents will be extinguished, so that they will need to find other links between each other for sustenance.

The second set of residential blocks in the To Kwa Wan section of the video—a group of twenty-two-story slabs organized perpendicular to the hillside—was developed by the nonprofit Hong Kong Housing Society in 1974 as an alternative to either public housing or private development. The Lok Man Sun Chuen estate begins north of Ko Shan Road Park and comprises more than 3,600 individual flats. The complex includes the Kei To Primary School and ten apartments for elderly residents needing medical care. One shot in Wong's video frames the wall of the primary school's interior courtyard, visible from the street; bouldering holds have been installed on the wall and the whole installation is painted a light blue (Figure 7). The balconies of the different tower slabs are marked by a graduated color scheme that begins as orange or green on lower floors and becomes increasingly pale as it ascends, creating a distinctive presence along the hillside.

Figure 7. The interior courtyard climbing wall of Kei To Primary School, part of the Lok Man Sun Chuen Housing Estate. Screenshot: Frame 22 of "When in Doubt, Take a Walk" (2020). Copyright © Sampson Wong.

The quality of this attention is also conveyed in the film, with shots that frame careful architectural decisions: the graduated façade, a monumental exterior stair, an entranceway with square tiles that pick up colors of an adjacent stone wall and the sky above. While these shots recall how public housing developments have become some of the most photographed and disseminated sites in Hong Kong—Instagrammable—the video's attention does not reproduce the vantage points and views of those circulated images, but instead offers new ways of looking at the constituted environment.

Cut into these scenes are views into the distance of the private towers that offer the most ubiquitous alternative to either the co-operative model of earlier decades or Lok Man Sun Chuen's nongovernmental, social housing. Interspersed as well are shots of solitary residents appropriating outdoor spaces as part of their day: one man carries a bird cage; another sits on concrete benches near a boundary wall; Wong walks by chairs hung, stacked, and arranged beside a fence, waiting in place for a time when it is possible to all meet again.[32]

The leisure and water infrastructures that comprise the third part of the video are an explicit expression of the government's investment in the well-being of its people: tennis courts, exercise equipment, a playing ground, and reservoirs for water storage and distribution. The configuration of elements in the penultimate shot—Wong sitting on a bench sipping his vending-machine drink with recycling bins nearby and rags hung to dry on the tennis-court fence—brings infrastructural systems into relation. That this is a moment of rest, speaks to the way this space in the city makes possible that resourcing. In retracing and examining Wong's trajectory through the different spaces of the video, we see infrastructural support everywhere.

But coming as it does after the Anti-ELAB protests, we could also consider how this trajectory enters into relation with events that are no longer present. Indeed, on September 9, 2019, in the midst of multiple actions throughout the city, secondary school children from neighborhood institutions in and near To Kwa Won formed a human chain along Ma Tau Wai Road: one of many human chain segments created in different parts of the city by school children.[33] The students were assembled in an intimate formation of human connection along city streets, speaking to an explicit link between human and material infrastructures, and the way such connection becomes a mechanism for the distribution of an affective response to the events taking place. To Kwa Wan was also the site of police response. One block from the Ko Shan Road bus stop where Wong begins his trajectory, nongovernmental organizations reported the use of tear gas on November 18 and November 11, respectively.[34] These responses took place during weeks of some of fiercest clashes between the government's security forces and protesters occupying the Hong Kong Polytechnic University—about a thirty-five-minute walk from Wong's chosen site. A few weeks earlier, on October 27, CableTV News reported another instance of tear gas use on their Telegram channel in the plaza fronting To Kwa Wan's main transit stop.[35]

The proximity of these events to the sites we see in Wong's video is, in some sense, not exceptional because of the ubiquity of both protest actions and government responses. Indeed, mapping projects identify protest events in Hong Kong Island, Kowloon, outlying districts, the airport, and in the New Territories close to the Hong Kong's border with Shenzen; tear gas incidents track almost 1:1 with the sites of protests.[36] This all-overness means that Wong's trajectory through the city, and the trajectory of subsequent videos, comes into contact with streets, subways tunnels, shopping malls, esplanades, and overpasses that were spatially implicated in protest. While traces of those events may no longer be present, they are never far and continue to mark the affective relationships—with the city, with each other, and with infrastructures—of those who call it home.

Conclusion

This recent history becomes an ambivalent heritage that is not resolved through walking, but rather reaffirmed in its implication with the city. Walking becomes a sustaining inscription of infrastructural trajectories that, in Berlant's terms, "binds us to the world in movement and keeps the world practically bound to itself"; in other words, as an infrastructural practice, walking allows Wong and others to hold on to difficult attachments with the expectation that this provisioning will make it possible to make it through to the softening of solidity's semblance. There is ambivalence about the emptying of life wrought by COVID-19 and the National Security Law yet also a recognition that uncertainty only makes love's attachment felt more sharply.

What is more, "When in Doubt" offers a reframing of heritage that functions through these different terms as a carrying forward of loss into the future. As a recollection of heritage, the video recasts a relation between past and future to describe a suspended "meanwhile" in which it is the *making it through* that becomes of value. We can understand this sentiment through the uncertainty that Berlant describes as an often glossed over aspect of the common: what is shared between is always striated with conflict, disagreements, and doubts that call for negotiation. What is common as heritage is never easy and invokes loss at the same time that it is a resource. It is this very notion of agonism that Hong Kong's government has sought to eradicate with NSL-supported moves to detain opposition leaders and civil society activists. Those arguing for a better way of organizing the social realm, and demanding to contribute to a discussion, are instead silenced for fomenting discontent.

"When in Doubt" provisions for the future of those who walk, for those who like & share, and potentially for others who come to know the city only later. The YouTube videos act as documents that allow routes traced through the city to memorialize and transmit a time that would otherwise be erased. Video, in this instance, stands in for the role of exposition or poetry—Hessel or Robertson—becoming a method for passing down but also enacting and documenting an affective relationship to streets, buildings, passageways, and people: infrastructure both as the conduits of circulation and as the sociality that supports and binds to the world. In walking, "When in Doubt," seeks to maintain a fragile heritage of social and political upheaval in Hong Kong's history as a place, city, and home. It functions not simply as a memorial, but as an infrastructural potential—a movement of life—that provisions.

Biography
Sony Devabhaktuni teaches architecture in the Art Program at Swarthmore College. His research focuses on urban infrastructures and collaborative processes in design with a particular concern for how economic, social, and political intensities overlap with imaginations of space. His writing has appeared in the *Architectural Theory Review*, *Public Culture*, *Global Performance Studies*, and the *AA Files*. His book *Curb-scale Hong Kong: Infrastructures of the Street* uses drawing and writing to describe the social and material relations that articulate the street as a shared realm in the context of the 2019 Anti-ELAB protests.

Notes
I thank two anonymous reviewers for their comments on an earlier draft of this text. The paper began as a talk for the Dance Studies Association 2022 Annual Conference: "Dancing Resilience: Dance Studies and Activism in a Global Age" and developed in sessions organized by the Department of Architecture at the University of Hong Kong and the Swarthmore College Art Program. My thanks to Tao Sule DuFour,

Lu Xiaoxuan, Joanna Mansbridge, Eunice Seng and Guillaume Othernîn-Girard for their input at various points in the writing.

[1] Sampson Wong, "When in doubt, just go," YouTube (2020–present), https://www.youtube.com/doubtwalk. The original name of the channel was "When in doubt, take a walk."

[2] Since British colonial occupation, "democracy and freedom" have been cast as secondary to the government's legitimizing, socioeconomic appeals for "prosperity and stability." See John D. Wong, "Constructing the Legitimacy of Governance in Hong Kong: 'Prosperity and Stability' Meets 'Democracy and Freedom,'" *Asian Studies* 81, no. 1 (2022): 43–61.

[3] For example, Occupy Central with Love and Peace in 2013, or the Umbrella Movement protests of 2014. The most comprehensive contemporaneous analysis of the Anti-ELAB protests can be found by the authors of the Lausan Collective. See Lausan Collective, https://lausancollective.com/?s=Anti+ELAB.

[4] Protests took place not only in the street or in outdoor plazas but also in the privately managed spaces of shopping malls and transit stations. This spatial and temporal diffusion was linked to the use of different mobile platforms that made nearly instantaneous coordination and response possible. See Ting Tin-yuet, "Opposing Otherness in Motion: Mobile Activism as Transient Heterotopia of Resistance in Hong Kong's Networked Mall Protests," *Geoforum* 136 (November 2022): 2–31.

[5] Katherine Whitworth and Yao-Tai Li discuss how the Lennon Walls became a site for the expression of sentiments toward both the protests and COVID-19 to mobilize the specificity of Hong Kong identity in relation to mainland China. See Katherine Whitworth and Yao-Tai Li, "Visual Framing: The Use of COVID-19 in the Mobilization of Hong Kong Protest," *The China Quarterly* 253 (November 4, 2022): 19–34.

[6] Wong is a lecturer in the Urban Studies Programme and the Department of Geography and Resource Management at the Chinese University of Hong Kong. Founder of several collectives that work at the intersection of art and protest, Wong also contributed a weekly newspaper column to Hong Kong–based *Ming Pao* and from 2017–20 hosted "Learning to Be a Social-scientist" on the "Weekday Night Forum," a talk show on RTHK, Hong Kong's public radio station. Wong began the YouTube channel, when he was dismissed from the show.

[7] Sampson Wong, "Notes on Hope and Urban-Walking Enthusiasm in Hong Kong," Critical Asia Archives (June 2023), https://caarchives.org/notes-on-hope-and-urban-walking-enthusiasm/. For some time, Wong dedicated his weekly *Ming Pao* column to people deciding to leave the city. Called "Let's Go Here First Before I Go" Wong would invite an acquaintance with plans to emigrate to experience a place, meal or walk that they had never undertaken in their time in Hong Kong. For Wong, the decision not to leave Hong Kong is in part explained by a deep affection for the city—what he describes in "Notes on Hope," citing Tuan Yi Fu, as "topophilia." See Tuan Yi Fu, *Topophilia: A Study of Environmental Perceptions, Attitudes and Values* (New York: Columbia University Press, 1990).

[8] Wong, "When in Doubt."

[9] See, for example, "M: The Flaneur," Walter Benjamin and Rolf Tiedemann, *The Arcades Project* (Cambridge, MA: Belknap Press, 1999), 416–55. Guy Débord, "Theory of the Dérive," from *Internationale Situationniste,* no. 2 (December 1958), https://libcom.org/article/theory-derive-guy-debord. Michel de Certeau, *The Practice of Everyday Life*, trans. Steven F. Rendall (Berkeley: University of California Press, 1984), 103.

[10] Injeong Yoon-Ramirez, "Walking-Sensing as a Decolonial Art and Pedagogical Practice" *International Journal of Education Through Art* 17, no. 1 (2021): 116.

[11] Yoon-Ramirez, "Walking-Sensing," 116.

[12] Carol Becker, "Walking, Standing, Sitting Like a Duck: Three Instances of Invasive, Reparative Behaviour," *Performance Research* 13, no. 3 (2008): 139–45.

[13] David Pinder, "Errant Paths: The Poetics and Politics of Walking," *Environment and Planning D, Society & Space* 29, no. 4 (2011): 684.

[14] Franz Hessel, *Walking in Berlin*, trans. Amanda DeMarco (Cambridge, MA: MIT Press, 2017.

[15] Lisa Robertson, *Occasional Work & Seven Walks from the Office for Soft Architecture* (Astoria: Clear Cut Press, 2003), 223–71.

[16] Lauren Berlant, "The Commons: Infrastructures for Troubling Times," *Environment and Planning D: Society and Space* 34, no. 3 (2016): 393, https://doi.org/10.1177/0263775816645989. This essay was first given as a talk to the American Association of Geographers annual meeting in 2015 and later became a chapter in the posthumously published book *On the Inconvenience of Other People* (2022).

[17] Susan Leigh Star, "The Ethnography of Infrastructure," *The American Behavioral Scientist* 43, no. 3 (1999): 377–91.

[18] See Brian Larkin, "The Politics and Poetics of Infrastructure," *Annual Review of Anthropology* 42, no. 1 (2013): 327–43.

[19] Berlant, "The Commons," 394.
[20] Berlant, "The Commons," 394. Italics in original.
[21] Berlant, "The Commons," 394. For comparison, "infrastructure" first appeared in debates in the French parliament about the construction of rail lines. "Infrastructure" was defined as engineering and sitework that needed to take place as a prerequisite support for what came afterwards: the placing of rail-lines and stations. Berlant's redefining of the two terms, challenges the hierarchy between them, foregrounding both infrastructure's life sustaining capacity, and its role as an agent of structure's transformation.
[22] Berlant, "The Commons," 393.
[23] Berlant, "The Commons," 394. Berlant considers Liza Johnson's film *In the Air* (2009) and Juliana's Spahr's poem "This Connection of Everyone with Lungs" (2005) as examples of "critical social form."
[24] Berlant, "The Commons," 394.
[25] Berlant, "The Commons," 394.
[26] Berlant, "The Commons," 395.
[27] Berlant, "The Commons," 395.
[28] Berlant, "The Commons," 395.
[29] Berlant, "The Commons," 395.
[30] This transformation has been led by the quasi-governmental Urban Reveal Authority, a profit-making body charged by the administration to seek out land deemed suitable for private development. In December of 2023, a consortium led by Sino-Land won development rights to the site with a bid of $272 million US dollars. See Daniel Ren, "Sino-Land led consortium snaps up Ma Tau Wai site despite worries about Hong Kong's sluggish economy and weak property market," *South China Morning Post*, December 14, 2023. https://www.scmp.com/business/companies/article/3245108/sino-land-led-consortium-snaps-ma-tau-wai-site-despite-worries-about-hong-kongs-sluggish-economy-and.
[31] Lawrence Wai Chung Lai, Kong Wing Chau, and Jason Wai Yin Kwong, "Surrendering the Environment for Capital Gain and Olson's Group Theory: A Case Study of the Dissolution of Housing Co-Operative Societies in Hong Kong." *Habitat International* 36, no. 2 (2012): 263. On possibilities for renewing cooperative housing models in Hong Kong, see: Guillaume Othenîn-Girard and Kent Mundle, "By Us, For Us: Hong Kong Cooperatives, Future Proof Narratives," *HKIA Journal* [*Community*] 79 (2024): 56–61.
[32] These frames recall the German photographer Michael Wolf's documentation of chairs in Hong Kong's alleyways, courtyards and entrances. The shared aesthetic suggests the ways in which Wong's video is informed by a careful and informed looking. See Michael Wolf, *Hong Kong Informal Seating Arrangements* (Berlin: Peperoni Books, 2014).
[33] Google Map, "Hong Kong Protests 2019–2020: Locations of Hong Kong Protests from March 31, 2019, to Present," October 13, 2013, https://bit.ly/3UGERhm. For reporting on the secondary school human chains that references the neighborhood, see Holmes Chan, "High school students form 'human chain' in support of Hong Kong protest movement," *Hong Kong Free Press* (September 9, 2019), https://hongkongfp.com/2019/09/09/high-school-students-form-human-chain-in-support-of-hong-kong-protest-movement/.
[34] The Hong Kong Free Press used "data reported on the official Telegram channels of eight media organizations and 84 other Telegram channels operated by protesters or political organizations from June 12, 2019, to March 21, 2020." In total the site identified 2,523 instances of tear gas being fired. See Hong Kong Free Press, "Hong Kong Protest Movement Data Archive: Tear Gas Map," last accessed February 2, 2024, https://hongkongfp.com/hong-kong-protest-movement-data-archive-tear-gas-map/.
[35] Hong Kong Free Press, "Tear Gas Map," last accessed February 2, 2024.
[36] Hong Kong Free Press, "Tear Gas Map," last accessed February 2, 2024.

Visa Immonen

Heritage Imagination as a Spatial Practice, and the Possibility of Alternative Futures

Introduction

The term "future," referring to something that will be or is expected to be, appears frequently in administrative and official texts where heritage is valued, protected, conserved, and cherished. Conservation and presentation of heritage are justified by appealing to future generations, or the future in general,[1] but at the same time future is often seen as a manageable progress occurring at heritage sites.[2] In contrast, Rodney Harrison, analyzing heritage practices and discourse, argues that future in activities related to heritage should be conceptualized as "worlding," a reality-establishing exercise that brings together material, semiotic, and social dimensions of reality.[3] As worlding, heritage practices are essentially coupled with the future as a future-oriented and future-shaping set of procedures and intentions. Heritage management plans govern which entities will be selected as prized items of the past, the shape and form these will take, and the medium or media through which they will be passed on. These practices are based on presuppositions about how the future will or should unfold. In this article, I follow the idea of worlding and argue that these future-making practices are inextricably intertwined with the spatiality of heritage. Their intimate relation is revealed through the concept of "heritage imagination," and I therefore suggest that this concept is fundamental for allowing future to emerge and opening novel spaces for heritage.

Future has preoccupied heritage experts both as the object of heritage analysis, and the agent of change. Cornelius Holtorf and Anders Höberg call for research to be carried out on the future-creating aspect of heritage and heritage management.[4] Another scholarly take on future is to go beyond analyzing the future envisioned by heritage institutions and established actors, and instead, try to discover and cultivate alternative heritage futures.[5] The rationale of such a transformative gesture is to shake off the unethical and harmful baggage of the modern life from heritage, including colonialism, racism, and the destruction of the environment, and orient us toward heritage futures that do not repeat or facilitate such atrocities.

The critical take on heritage futures springs partly from the unrestrained accumulation of modernity's heritage as the relics of human and biological life: diminishing biodiversity, toxic waste, the crumbling ruins of concrete buildings and

Future Anterior
Volume XX, Numbers 1–2
Summer / Winter 2023

the vanishing life patterns of minority communities.[6] These pose the question of how we are to cope with this pernicious legacy as our heritage. In a similar vein, the world-transforming phenomenon of the Anthropocene, referring to the planetary-level amalgamation of humankind and the non-human world, challenges the future envisioned and anticipated by established heritage practices, a future that is no longer ethically or existentially viable. The Anthropocene requires a new kind of conception of heritage while forcing us to think about how heritage can contribute to the emergence of alternative futures.

In analyzing the future anticipated within heritage texts and communities, and in envisioning new futures, many heritage scholars draw inspiration from similar discussions in anthropology and ethnology, social sciences, and contemporary philosophy.[7] The words "imagination" and "re-imagination" occur frequently in this corpus of work as a means to formulate alternative futures. For instance, Donna Haraway stresses the importance of cultivating "response-ability" in the Anthropocene, and points out "the high stakes of training the mind and imagination to go visiting, to venture off the beaten path to meet unexpected, non-natal kin, to strike up conversations, to pose and respond to interesting questions, to propose together something unanticipated, and to take up unasked-for obligations of having met."[8] Imagination and future-making coexist, and for scholarship on heritage, imagination appears to guarantee the creation of something completely novel with relation to what presently exists, including the ruins of modernity.

In this article, I also approach heritage from the perspective of embodied and spatializing imagination,[9] but argue that imagination does not, in fact, inevitably engender novel futures without sharper theoretical refinement and acknowledging the fundamental connection of imagination with spatiality. To accomplish such conceptual precision, I first analyze the use of imagination in other disciplines. In 1959, C. Wright Mills introduced the concept of "sociological imagination,"[10] provoking a series of other disciplinary imaginations: geographical,[11] anthropological,[12] antiquarian,[13] ethnological,[14] and archaeological.[15] I approach this transdisciplinary conceptual exchange as disciplinary heritage. It combines the notion of "imagination" with each discipline's respective characteristics and uses this as a steppingstone to go beyond the state of the art. It also reveals the spatiotemporal imagination in Heritage Studies, sometimes argued to be an inter- or non-discipline.[16]

After a disciplinary analysis, I move on to the tradition of philosophy to gain a better view on the workings of imagination as spatializing faculty. Imagination is grounded in our bodily existence. Consequently, on the one hand, heritage imagination sketches out a form of imagination specific for, and effective in, scholarship on heritage; on the other hand, it shows how difficult it actually is to be creatively imaginative. In fact, imagining alternative heritage futures might signify the task of clearing away ideas and traditions, come into terms with them, rather than generating seemingly new ones, in order to open up spaces for fresh thought and action. Moreover, heritage imagination is of relevance to academics, educators, practitioners, and policymakers alike, because the concept shows that discussions on the future of heritage should not be limited to high-level vision papers and policy statements, which, in fact, tend to enforce present preconceptions and predispositions as the future. Instead, alternative futures for heritage are created through our bodily practices and in relationship with everyday spatial arrangements, and therefore imagining alternative and better futures is never restricted to experts alone.

The Launch of Disciplinary Imaginations

In his seminal work on sociological imagination, Mills calls attention to the "troubles" that an ordinary person faces in the modern world.[17] These problems are often accepted as individual and isolated issues because people do not have "the quality of mind" to understand the connection between themselves and society, or between biography and history.[18] Mills names this ability "sociological imagination," as it enables the analysis of personal difficulties in relation to others and social structures. In fact, sociological imagination is "the major common denominator of our cultural life and its signal feature,"[19] and thus requires cultivation and dissemination.[20]

Sociological imagination is a faculty stemming from everyday life, but developed within a disciplinary context, and then applied to make sense of an initial experience. Mills distinguishes sociological imagination from two trends prevalent in the sociology of his time. First, it does not consider "social science as a set of bureaucratic techniques," which present sociological imagination as a positivistic or technocratic endeavor. Second, since sociological imagination derives from the commonplace, it is an antidote to abstract theoretical work that has no connection with everyday experience.[21] According to Mills, developing this kind of sensibility requires an expansion of the awareness of one's own experience, and thus sociological imagination demands a playfulness of mind, combining apparently incompatible ideas to create socially valuable insights.[22] To achieve this, sociological imagination "consists of the capacity to shift from one perspective to another, and in the process to build up an adequate view of a total society and of its components."[23]

The ideas that Mills proposed regarding sociological imagination were adopted in other disciplines. Hugh C. Prince coined the term "geographical imagination" in 1962,[24] arguing that an aesthetic sensibility to landscape and nature is a universal instinct, not confined to the academic discipline of human geography. He considered the commingling of culture with nature in everyday experience as a creative act expressed in geographical descriptions. David Harvey expands Prince's views by shifting the emphasis from nature and culture to the concepts of place and space. He states that geographical imagination enables to recognize the role of spatiality in our lives and use space creatively.[25]

Mills established a tradition that gave coherence to how different disciplinary imaginations have been construed since. These commence with everyday experiences that have become the object of our imagination. Imagination is thus a collectively shared faculty, not reserved for certain exceptional individuals.[26] However, imagination does not solely consist of detecting and making connections between entities within our experience. Instead, scholarly cultivation is required to develop findings into knowledge and assist in understanding each initial experience. Although based on claims of scholarly rigor, disciplinary imaginations maintain an anti-bureaucratic attitude, emphasizing a cultural or historical perspective. They help to navigate in the contemporary world.[27]

Postmodernist and Historical Complications

In the 1990s, against a backdrop of pluralization of scholarly voices and the rise of postmodernist theories, some of the suppositions made in the tradition of disciplinary imaginations came into question. This was most prevalent within human geography, where it was argued that geography and its epistemology are not only a reflection of the world, as previously assumed, but that these also serve to construct reality and our attitudes to space and place. Geographical imagination did more than merely cultivate something that already existed,[28] and the once-fixed divide between the object and subject of scholarship was exposed as blurred. For instance, Derek Gregory argues that the habits of mind advocated by Prince and Harvey represent and reinforce a white, masculine, and Eurocentric worldview.[29] Postcolonial critique has also pointed out similar problems within sociological imagination.[30] Consequently, disciplinary imaginations are not uniform units, but each consist of nonacademic and academic imaginations with indistinct boundaries.

These theoretical shifts continue to influence the adaptation of disciplinary imaginations in the twenty-first century. For Fuyuki Kurasawa, the impetus of "ethnological imagination" is not aimed at the discipline and its transformation, but rather at exposing a counter current in modern European thought. The concept refers to mythical representations of non-Western societies in the Western corpus of thought. Kurasawa shows how Western thinkers construct an intercultural gaze, and direct it to Western societies and thereby ethnologize, defamiliarize, and denaturalize the Euro-American forms of thinking and conduct. He points out that, on the one hand, such instrumental uses of non-Western cultures are problematic and frequently based on a flawed understanding of other cultures but, on the other hand, such counterpoints do provide a way to foster self-critique.[31]

History is another discipline for which heritage imagination is relevant, and "historical imagination" appears frequently within the philosophy of history. The definition and usage of the concept, however, differs markedly from those of the other disciplines. This is because the word "history" is semantically broader than, for instance, sociology or geography, and here resembles the term "heritage." It does not denote solely an academic discipline but refers broadly to all narratives relating to the past. Consequently, the applications of historical imagination are not all related to this scholarly discipline or how to conduct it appropriately. For instance, the concept can be applied to describe how a certain a group of people viewed the past at a certain period in time.

Although no theoretician of history denies the presence of, or even the need for, imagination in the writing of history, views vary on its significance to claims of historical veracity. R. G. Collingwood,[32] for instance, states that historical inquiry and reconstruction require imagination. Meanwhile, Hayden White controversially argues that historical imagination is close to, or even conditioned by, literary constructs used for narrating events.[33] After White, the concept itself has, for some scholars, come to symbolize the postmodern rejection of historical truth and its dependence upon source evidence.[34] In sum, historical imagination stems from a separate tradition to that of other disciplinary imaginations. It is concerned with probing the disciplinary limits of imagination and, in doing so, setting its discipline's claims to truthfulness on a firmer basis. This manner of employing the concept is a reminder that other forms of disciplinary imaginations are also based on implicit or explicit criteria and practices that set them apart from non-disciplinary modes of conveying knowledge.

Imagination within Philosophical Tradition

Mills's sociological imagination presented a vision of the state of the art within sociology and how to transform society with the tools provided by this discipline. Mills taps into the creative promise of imagination but engages less pointedly with its definition and conceptual history, and the same terminological sketchiness characterizes other disciplinary imaginations as well. This is unfortunate, because Western philosophy has analyzed imagination since Antiquity,[35] and these insights are useful in scrutinizing the relationship between imagination, spatiality, and the future.

Etymologically the word "imagination" derives from the Latin noun "image," *imago*. This linguistic history has framed European philosophical engagement with the concept, as imagination is frequently considered as a simulation or creation of novel sensations and ideas in the mind, without any immediate perception.[36] For modern philosophy, Immanuel Kant's work forms the basis for the analysis of imagination, and in general terms, he places imagination at the core of thinking.[37] In experience, Kant distinguishes three functions of the mind, which process percepts, or sensory inputs, for conceptual thinking: sensibility (intuition), imagination (reproduction) and understanding (recognition). To become intelligible, our experience requires both percepts and concepts, with imagination serving as the mediator between these two. Reproduction or imagination connects percepts to form an image of reality for our understanding to process.[38] In imagination, earlier sensory percepts are retained so that together with earlier representations they bring about "a transition of the mind."[39]

Crucially, fulfilling such a representational function is only the first aspect of imagination in Kant's view. In fact, the second aspect gives imagination a more constitutive role in cognition. Imagination still acts as a mediator, but no longer serves merely as an aid toward understanding.[40] Kant writes that imagination is an "indispensable function of the soul, without which we would have no cognition at all, but of which we are seldom even conscious."[41] He explains that imagination is the concealed condition for all knowledge because it is "the faculty for representing an object even without its presence in" perception, and this allows the mind to free itself from the confines of percepts.[42] Imagination thus becomes the basis for all thought and frees us from the limits of perception.[43]

Phenomenology continues the tradition of examining imagination as a sensory and bodily experience of something that is not immediately present.[44] According to Edmund Husserl, imagining is an experience of inactuality, and thus quasi-perceptual in the sense that the imagined object, although not present, has a sensory content, and that the subject's intention is directed toward it.[45] In other words, there is no fundamental cut between the perception and imagined objects. Nonetheless, imagined entities appear always as represented and possible, not actual, and thus the act of imagination remains separate from perception.

Breaking with earlier tradition, however, Husserl strongly rejects the understanding of imagination in terms of "mental images," or as visual representations formed within the mind, in opposition to objects existing outside it.[46] For Husserl, imagination is a matter of actively simulating possible, embodied experiences of imagined objects. It is by means of the imagination that from "every concrete actuality, and every individual trait actually experienced in it or capable of being experienced, a path stands open to the real of ideal or pure possibility and consequently to that of *a priori* thinking."[47]

On the concept of pure possibility, Maurice Merleau-Ponty states that, like real objects, imagined ones always appear as something to somebody, and thus imagination becomes a form of attending the possible in the real. Since the possible permeates everything, reality and its comprehension are always both perceptual and imaginary. In Merleau-Ponty's view, perception, embodied spatiality, and imagination are interlinked, establishing a dialectic between the actual and the possible.[48]

In developing the idea of possibilities, Edward Casey makes a distinction between imagining hypothetical possibilities and imagining pure possibilities. Hypothetical possibilities refer to entities as though they were actual or real, as when we anticipate the restoration of a building that is yet to be completed. In contrast, pure possibility is entirely cut off from the facts of reality, and could involve, for instance, envisioning what heritage means to other lifeforms than humans, or what it will signify after the present environmental crisis. The modality of pure possibility is the condition for creativity and freedom, whether in academia or the arts.[49]

Importantly, through the concept of imagination, freedom becomes related to indeterminacy. Casey argues that the "more indeterminate something is or appears to be, the more it will tend to present itself as purely possible; and the more purely possible something is or appears to be, the greater the tendency for it to be indeterminate in form."[50] However, as Merleau-Ponty points out, imagining pure possibilities does not mean giving up the reality or the facticity of our embodied existence entirely: "[O]n the contrary, it is the possible worlds and possible things that are variants and doubles of the actual world and of actual beings."[51] Imagining thus retains its crucial connection to human spatial experience.

New Materialist Revision

Phenomenology distrusts the theory of imagination as a faculty that generates mental images but has not dispensed with the notion of representation entirely. Similarly, it has explored and emphasized the creative aspect of imagination, yet, as Merleau-Ponty writes, imagination is still said to be rooted in our embodied relationship with the actual world. These aspects are the points of criticism upon which new materialist strands of thought have concentrated, arguing that phenomenology does not go far enough. This calls into question the potential of imagination to generate any substantial transformation, or alternative futures. Such rejections of the phenomenological approach derive largely from Gilles Deleuze's and Félix Guattari's work.[52]

Criticizing Sigmund Freud's psychoanalysis and the Oedipus myth, Deleuze and Guattari write that "[d]esiring-production is personalized, or rather personologized (*personnologisée*), imaginarized (*imaginarisée*), structuralized [. . .]. Production is reduced to mere fantasy production, production of expression."[53] Such a stance toward the imaginary stems from their wider philosophical project to replace the psychoanalytical conception of desire, as a sense of want or lack, with the notion of a productive desire. This also means dismantling the idea of thinking as representational or as a play of images and signs standing for something that is absent or lacking. When conveyed in this manner, thinking becomes dictated by what can be represented and already distanced from reality, and therefore loses its ability to be radically productive.[54] Against this background, it is not surprising that imagination becomes problematic.

Deleuze proposes an alternative approach to human thought, not as a faculty for generating and processing images, but based on encounters. Encounters entail more than one entity (the human mind) and thus thinking becomes a situation in which these different entities affect each other materially and send each other in new directions. Each encounter sparks a productive desire to make sense of and create new concepts. In Deleuze's view, imagination, limited to images and reality, is not the instigator of such an encounter or a radical transformation. Instead, true thinking is something which we cannot imagine, something to which we cannot respond without creating something new. Consequently, imagination, which is distinct from thinking, is not capable of generating alternative futures.[55]

Although the role of imagination seems rather bleak, Erik Bormanis suggests that it can be salvaged if it is conceived, like desire, as a productive force. He points out that for Deleuze, a crucial aspect of thinking is the opening of a space for encounters, or the securing of conditions for exploration. These gestures of clearing up mean, for instance, destroying old images and structures to allow a proper encounter to occur. For imagination to be productive it must engage in the act of cleaning mental images away. This leads to imagining without images. In Bormanis's solution, imagination remains connected with reality and our embodied being but moves from the imagination of hypothetical possibilities toward the imagination of pure possibilities. To achieve this, imagination must flush out old representations, allowing for a new set of percepts to appear. Such radical alterity is, however, hard to attain and remains transitory, since once-novel percepts will turn into clichés and hinder further imaginative encounters.[56]

In European philosophy, imagination has been identified as a faculty of the mind that generates mental images without immediate percepts from reality. Kant developed the idea of imagination as a mediator between sensory impressions, but also suggested that imagination is a condition for all understanding. The phenomenological tradition subscribes to this view but questions the idea of imagination as a faculty based on mental images. Instead, Husserl considers imagination as an embodied experience, a certain temporal and spatial way of orienting oneself toward the world, while Merleau-Ponty argues that imagination and perception are interwoven, with imagination cherishing the possible in the actual. This rejection of the image theory of imagination culminates in Deleuze's and Guattari's work. Based on their theories, a viable understanding of imagination should embrace pure possibility and posit imagination as a process of dismantling images. This underscores that imagination has a complex and context-dependent relationship with the actual and the possible.

Heritage Imagination

The philosophical tradition relating to imagination can be transferred to the context of disciplinary imaginations, which will, in effect, help to define the scope of heritage imagination. The first term within heritage imagination, "heritage," refers to a discipline or rather a set of scholarly and management practices, as is the case for many other disciplinary imaginations. By contrast, however, its wide extent reveals an affinity with the notion of "historical imagination," covering both scholarly and non-scholarly, managerial and interpretative, aspects of heritage. Heritage is embedded into our everyday experiences as a set of objects, conceptions, and practices. It helps make sense of the modern life, and it orders and transforms reality, but can also become the object of disciplinary knowledge production and scholarly interventions.

When heritage becomes the object of imagination, this activity draws upon our embodied and spatialized experiences of the physical and conceptual expressions of heritage. It is thus not simply a matter of processing mental images but creation of space. This refers to monuments, sites, archives, and museum exhibitions as places of experience, and even more broadly to our bodily encounter of these places, and the spatial practices and politics which they induce. In fact, there is no single, uniform experience of heritage but, instead, experiences conditioned by a kaleidoscope of attitudes and heritage communities, each with their own specific spatiality and interests. In this multitude of spatial experiences, imagination operates in all forms of engagement with heritage, from imagining hypothetical possibilities to pure possibilities, or in other words, from making sense of heritage at hand to transforming it.

Although imagination is present in all our interactions with heritage, the motivation for introducing the concept of heritage imagination does not lie primarily in gaining new results through individual studies, but in the promise of grasping a novel understanding of heritage as radically spatial practice and its embodied relationship with heritage scholarship, and in envisaging novel ways of conceptualizing both. It is based on a disciplinary tradition that draws from transdisciplinary heritage. Furthermore, heritage imagination contains an assumption that knowledge produced on heritage is employed directly or indirectly to improve our environment and lives.

Heritage imagination as an anti-positivistic and holistic concept is a reminder that heritage covers issues of conservation, economy, management and law, but importantly also addresses questions of a conceptual, cultural, and social nature. Scholarship on heritage provides a broad set of practices and criteria as well as points of debate for engaging with heritage. In terms of its theories and methodologies, Heritage Studies might have more in common with archaeology, anthropology, ethnology, human geography, and sociology than with history, but the debate on historical imagination is important as it calls attention to the transdisciplinary context of heritage imagination. As a disciplinary practice, analyzing heritage establishes a certain framework for imagination, but simultaneously, open avenues for imagining things that would not otherwise be attainable.

Conclusion

After sketching out what heritage imagination means, I turn to examine the relationship between imagination, spatiality, and the future, and ask whether heritage imagination can produce alternative futures. In the philosophical discourse on imagination, its embodied structure is posited, and the distinction between hypothetical and pure possibilities is useful for teasing this out. These two kinds of possibilities describe the variety of effects that imagination can produce. Hypothetical possibilities—or entities imagined as if they were real—orient our movements and thinking when we anticipate or assume something to be actual or try to make it actual. A flow of such imaginations is constantly present in our actions. In contrast, pure possibilities—or imagined entities with no immediate connection to the actual—have a more intricate relationship with spatiality. As such imaginations are purely potential in nature, the imagined entities may appear as utopias or dystopias projected to the future, directing our actions to achieve the former and avoid the latter. Such imagined entities might reside beyond the experiences of our everyday life and still affect our spatial orientation. Whether imaginations are common or exceptional, they nonetheless condition our orientation to the environment in the present.

The spatiality of imagination is tied with creativity, spontaneity, and, ultimately, freedom. These become materialized in dialectics between the possible and the actual. Imagination works upon the real, attending or caring for the possibilities ingrained within it. According to Merleau-Ponty, imagination can never be free of its ties with the given, or the real, but still allows for the emergence of alternative percepts and notions. For Deleuze and Guattari, on the contrary, imagination's transformative force is hampered by its unavoidable ties with the real, especially when it is approached as the processing of mental images. Bormanis's reading, however, restores the ability of imagination to be productive if it is conceived of in terms of clearing up old images for something novel to appear and, subsequently, of allowing thinking to take place.

This philosophical analysis on the relationship between imagination and the future shows that the future is also present in heritage imagination. It conditions how we perceive and think, and it affects our embodied ways in which we live in the world. Consequently, even if discussions on heritage futures tend to approach spatiality in a highly abstracted fashion, for instance, as a matter of managerial ways to govern visitors or through such broad geological notions as the Anthropocene, heritage imagination and heritage futures are still grounded in human experience, in all its diversity and complexity. Remembering this groundedness might help to address the problem of modernity's heritage, and its constant, suffocating accumulation.

As emphasized by phenomenology, imagination and perception crisscross each other, and therefore imagination is present at all levels and in all forms of understanding and action. This implies that although heritage imagination also comes with a promise of alternative futures, all imaginings do not produce great transformations but are rather a routine part of life. However, the more imagination is oriented toward pure possibilities, the more indeterminate it becomes. Many discussions on imagination in the context of heritage assume that imagination produces results that are good, positive, and revitalizing. Such wishful thinking is based on our present-day aspirations, however, and that already bounds, and determines what imagination imagines. Yet imagination of pure possibilities and alternative futures cannot be tied to our anticipations if these are to maintain their creativity and novelty. Consequently, calls for fresh imaginings do not automatically lead to producing alternative futures, and in fact, they may confine imagination to repeat existing patterns of thought and bodily existence.

Heritage imagination underscores the intertwined nature of heritage management and non-institutionalized uses and interpretations of heritage. It reveals a connection between shaping and interpreting heritage as they are rooted in the embodied and spatial structures of the life world. Although both necessarily affect each other, their relationship remains conditioned by power relations. Alternative ways of experiencing heritage, like creating new walking paths across the heritage site, or telling alternate stories of the place, require identification and cultivation, or translation into the language of professionalism and management if they are to have the same impact and consideration as the already established practices. On the other hand, these nonprofessional uses and perceptions are steeped with clichés of their own kind, and even the translation work involves banalities and making the alternative into something traditional, like the off-the-beaten-track tourists who often pave the way for mass tourism.[57] Finding and creating alternative futures is not a goal but a constantly transmuting activity which encompasses all aspects of heritage.

To the extent that imagination is a prerequisite for creativity, it also serves as a basis for both utopic and dystopic visions of reality. Meanwhile, as Deleuze and Guattari point out, imagination is not an unproblematic way to try to attain alternative futures. To achieve these might require not so much the conception of seemingly new and untamed projections, but rather the creation of a space for thinking and for the emergence of indeterminate futures and their heritage. Hence, in the majority of cases, the most future-oriented action available is not to present a bold, futuristic heritage utopia, but to open a space for thinking and alternative heritage futures, and it is in this task that heritage imagination finds its true calling.

Biography
Visa Immonen is Professor of Archaeology at the University of Bergen, Norway. Much of his work focuses on medieval material culture in the Nordic countries, but he is also interested in Heritage Studies. He has examined, for instance, the community of metal detectorists, the practice of taking nude selfies at heritage sites, and queer heritage.

Notes

[1] Robert Hewison, "Heritage: An Interpretation," in *Heritage Interpretation: Vol. I: The Natural and Built Environment*, ed. David L. Uzzell (London: Belhaven, 1989), 16; J. E. Tunbridge and G. J. Ashworth, *Dissonant Heritage: The Management of the Past as a Resource in Conflict* (Chichester: Wiley, 1996), 6.

[2] For example, Dirk H. R. Spennemann, "Of Great Apes and Robots: Considering the Future(s) of Cultural Heritage," *Futures* 39, no. 7 (2007): 861–77; Rodney Harrison, Nadia Bartolini, Caitlin DeSilvey, Cornelius Holtorf, Antony Lyons, Sharon MacDonald, Sarah May, Jennie Morgan, and Sefryn Penrose, "Heritage Futures,"

Archaeology International 19, no. 1 (2016), https://doi.org/10.5334/ai.1912; Anders Högberg, Cornelius Holtorf, Sarah May, and Gustav Wollentz, "No Future in Archaeological Heritage Management?," *World Archaeology* 49, no. 5 (2017): 639–47; Rodney Harrison, Caitlin DeSilvey, Cornelius Holtorf, Sharon MacDonald, Nadia Bartolini, Esther Breithoff, Harald Fredheim, Antony Lyons, Sarah May, Jennie Morgan, and Sefryn Penrose, eds., *Heritage Futures: Comparative Approaches to Natural and Cultural Heritage Practices* (London: UCL Press, 2020); Cornelius Holtorf and Anders Högberg, eds., *Cultural Heritage and the Future* (New York: Routledge, 2021). The interest in heritage futures follows a similar trend in disciplines like anthropology and archaeology. See, e.g., Juan Francisco Salazar, Sarah Pink, Andrew Irving, and Johannes Sjöberg, eds., *Anthropologies and Futures: Researching Emerging and Uncertain Worlds* (London: Bloomsbury, 2017); Cornelius Holtorf and Anders Högberg, "Archaeology and the Future," in *Encyclopedia of Global Archaeology*, ed. Claire Smith (Cham: Springer, 2018); Rebecca Bryant and Daniel M. Knight, *The Anthropology of the Future* (Cambridge: Cambridge University Press, 2019), and draws from the increasing visibility and influence of Futures Studies within cultural and social studies; see, e.g., Richard A. Slaughter and Andy Hines, eds., *The Knowledge Base of Futures Studies 2020* (Brisbane: Foresight International, 2020).

[3] Rodney Harrison, "Heritage Practices as Future-Making Practices," in *Cultural Heritage and the Future*, ed. Cornelius Holtorf and Anders Högberg (London and New York: Routledge, 2021), 29–45.

[4] Cornelius Holtorf and Anders Högberg, "Introduction: Cultural Heritage as a Futuristic Field," in *Cultural Heritage and the Future*, ed. Cornelius Holtorf and Anders Högberg (New York: Routledge, 2021).

[5] Colin Sterling and Rodney Harrison, "Introduction: Of Territories and Temporalities," in *Deterritorializing the Future: Heritage in, of and after the Anthropocene*, ed. Rodney Harrison and Colin Sterling (London: Open Humanities Press, 2020), 29.

[6] Julia Hell and Andreas Schönle, eds., *Ruins of Modernity* (Durham, NC: Duke University Press, 2010); Anna Lowenhaupt Tsing, *The Mushroom at the End of the World: On the Possibility of Life in Capitalist Ruins* (Princeton, NJ: Princeton University Press, 2015); Anna Lowenhaupt Tsing, Heather Anne Swanson, Elain Gan, and Nils Bubandt, eds., *Arts of Living on a Damaged Planet: Ghosts of the Anthropocene: Monsters of the Anthropocene* (Minneapolis: University of Minnesota Press, 2017); Elizabeth Kryder-Reid and Sarah May, eds., *Toxic Heritage: Legacies, Futures, and Environmental Injustice* (London: Routledge, 2024).

[7] For example, Christina Fredengren, and Cecilia Åsberg, "Checking in with Deep Time: Intragenerational Care in Registers of Feminist Posthumanities, the Case of Gärstadsverken," in *Deterritorializing the Future: Heritage in, of and after the Anthropocene*, ed. Rodney Harrison and Colin Sterling (London: Open Humanities Press, 2020); Rodney Harrison and Colin Sterling, eds., *Deterritorializing the Future: Heritage in, of and after the Anthropocene* (London: Open Humanities Press, 2020); see also Emma Waterton and Steve Watson, "Framing Theory: Towards a Critical Imagination in Heritage Studies," *International Journal of Heritage Studies* 19, no. 6 (2013): 546–61.

[8] Donna Haraway, *Staying with the Trouble: Making Kin in the Chthulucene* (London: Duke University Press, 2016), 130.

[9] See, for example, Harrison and Sterling, *Deterritorializing the Future*.

[10] C. Wright Mills, *The Sociological Imagination* (New York: Oxford University Press, 1959).

[11] Hugh C. Prince, "The Geographical Imagination," *Landscape* 11 (1962): 22–25.

[12] Muriel Dimen-Schein, *The Anthropological Imagination* (New York: McGraw-Hill, 1977).

[13] Stuart Piggott, *Ancient Britons and the Antiquarian Imagination: Ideas from the Renaissance to the Regency* (New York: Thames and Hudson, 1989).

[14] Fuyuki Kurasawa, *The Ethnological Imagination: A Cross-Cultural Critique of Modernity* (Minneapolis: University of Minnesota Press, 2004).

[15] Jennifer Wallace, *Digging the Dirt: The Archaeological Imagination* (London: Duckworth, 2004); Michael Shanks, *The Archaeological Imagination* (London: Routledge, 2012).

[16] David Uzzell, "Where Is the Discipline in Heritage Studies? A View from Environmental Psychology," in *Heritage Studies: Methods and Approaches*, ed. Marie Louise Stig Sørensen and John Carman (London: Routledge, 2009).

[17] Mills, *The Sociological Imagination*, 3.

[18] Mills, *The Sociological Imagination*, 4.

[19] Mills, *The Sociological Imagination*, 13.

[20] Mills, *The Sociological Imagination*, 18; Tania Zittoun and Vlad Petre Glăveanu, "Imagination at the Frontiers of Psychology," in *Handbook of Imagination and Culture*, ed. Tania Zittoun and Vlad Petre Glăveanu (Oxford: Oxford University Press, 2018), 7.

[21] Mills, *The Sociological Imagination*, 20, 133.
[22] Mills, *The Sociological Imagination*, 166.
[23] Mills, *The Sociological Imagination*, 211.
[24] Prince, "The Geographical Imagination."
[25] David Harvey, *Social Justice and the City* (London: Edward Arnold, 1973), 23–24.
[26] Arjun Appadurai, "Grassroots Globalization and the Research Imagination," *Public Culture* 12, no. 1 (2000): 6.
[27] Shanks, *The Archaeological Imagination*, 27.
[28] Derek Gregory, *Geographical Imaginations* (Oxford: Blackwell, 1994); Rosalyn Deutsche, "Surprising Geography," *Annals of the Association of American Geographers* 85 (1995).
[29] Gregory, *Geographical Imaginations*; see also Gillian Rose, *Feminism and Geography: The Limits of Geographical Knowledge* (Cambridge: Polity, 1993); Deutsche, "Surprising Geography," *Annals of the Association of American Geographers*; Peter Jackson, "Constructions of "Whiteness' in the Geographical Imagination," *Area* 30, no. 2 (1998); Allan Pred, "Somebody Else, Somewhere Else: Racisms, Racialized Spaces and the Popular Geographical Imagination in Sweden," *Antipode* 29, no. 4 (2002).
[30] Gurminder K. Bhambra, *Rethinking Modernity: Postcolonialism and the Sociological Imagination* (Basingstoke and New York: Palgrave MacMillan, 2007); Martin Savransky, "A Decolonial Imagination: Sociology, Anthropology and the Politics of Reality," *Sociology* 51, no. 1 (2017).
[31] Kurasawa, *The Ethnological Imagination*.
[32] R. G. Collingwood, *The Idea of History* (Oxford: Oxford University Press, 1946), 232–49; William H. Dray, *History as Re-Enactment: R. G. Collingwood's Idea of History* (Oxford: Oxford University Press, 1995), 191–228.
[33] Hayden White, *Metahistory: The Historical Imagination in Nineteenth-Century Europe* (Baltimore: The Johns Hopkins University Press, 1973).
[34] For example, Jan Vansina, "Book Review: Ethnography and the Historical Imagination by Jean Comaroff and John Comaroff," *The International Journal of African Historical Studies* 26, no. 2 (1993): 417, note 1.
[35] Leslie Stevenson, "Twelve Conceptions of Imagination," *British Journal of Aesthetics* 43, no. 3 (2003): 238–59.
[36] For the conceptual history of imagination in premodern and early modern philosophy, see Edward Casey, "Imagining and Remembering," *The Review of Metaphysics* 31, no. 2 (1977); J. M. Cocking, *Imagination: A Study of the History of Ideas* (London: Routledge, 1991); Victor Caston, "Why Aristotle Needs Imagination," *Phronesis* 41, no. 1 (1996); David J. Staley, *Historical Imagination* (London: Routledge, 2021).
[37] Cocking, *Imagination*; John Rundell, "Creativity and Judgement: Kant on Reason and Imagination," in *Rethinking Imagination*, ed. Gillian Robinson and John Rundell (London: Routledge, 1994).
[38] Rudolf A. Makkreel, *Imagination and Interpretation in Kant: The Hermeneutical Import of the Critique of Judgment* (Chicago: The University of Chicago Press, 1990); Andrew Brook and Julian Wuerth, "Kant's View of the Mind and Consciousness of Self," in *Stanford Encyclopedia of Philosophy*, ed. Edward N. Zalta (Palo Alto: Stanford University, 2020).
[39] Immanuel Kant, *Critique of Pure Reason* (Cambridge: Cambridge University Press, 1998), 229.
[40] Martin Heidegger, *Kant and the Problem of Metaphysics* (Bloomington: Indiana University Press, 1997).
[41] Kant, *Critique of Pure Reason*, 211.
[42] Kant, *Critique of Pure Reason*, 256.
[43] Jodie Lee Heap, *The Creative Imagination: Indeterminacy and Embodiment in the Writings of Kant, Fichte and Castoriadis* (Landham, MD: Rowman & Littlefield, 2021).
[44] Edward Casey, Elizabeth A. Behnke, and Susumu Kanata, "Imagination," in *Encyclopedia of Phenomenology*, ed. Lester Embree, Elizabeth A. Behnke, David Carr, J. Claude Evans, Jose Huertas-Jourda, Joseph J. Kockemans, William R. McKenna, Algis Mickunas, Jitendra Nath Mohanty, Thomas M. Seebohm, and Richard M. Zaner (Dordrecht: Springer, 1997); see also Tao Dufour, *Husserl and Spatiality: A Phenomenological Ethnography of Space* (London: Routledge, 2022).
[45] Julia Jansen, "Phenomenology, Imagination and Interdisciplinary Research," in *Handbook of Phenomenology and Cognitive Science*, ed. Shaun Gallagher and Daniel Schmicking (Dordrecht: Springer, 2010).
[46] Edward Casey, *Imagining: A Phenomenological Study*, 2nd ed. (Bloomington: Indiana University Press, 2000).
[47] Edumund Husserl, *Experience and Judgement: Investigations in a Genealogy of Logic* (Evanston: Northwestern University Press, 1973), 353–54.
[48] Maurice Merleau-Ponty, *The Merleau-Ponty Aesthetics Reader* (Evanston: Northwestern University Press, 1993).

[49] Casey, *Imagining*, 103.
[50] Casey, *Imagining*, 103.
[51] Maurice Merleau-Ponty, *The Visible and the Invisible* (Evanston: Northwestern University Press, 1968), 112.
[52] Gilles Deleuze and Félix Guattari, *Anti-Oedipus: Capitalism and Schizophrenia* (Minneapolis: University of Minnesota Press, 1983).
[53] Deleuze and Guattari, *Anti-Oedipus*, 55.
[54] Gilles Deleuze, *Difference and Repetition* (New York: Columbia University Press, 1994); Gilles Deleuze and Félix Guattari, *What Is Philosophy?* (New York: Columbia University Press, 1994).
[55] Deleuze, *Difference and Repetition*.
[56] Erik Bormanis, "The Possibility of a Productive Imagination in the Work of Deleuze and Guattari," in *Imagination and Art: Explorations in Contemporary Theory*, ed. Keith Moser, and Ananta Ch. Sukla (Leiden and Boston: Brill, 2020).
[57] Sabrina Seeler, Michael Lück, and Heike Schänzel, "Paradoxes and Actualities of Off-the-beaten-track Tourists," *Journal of Hospitality and Tourism Management* 53 (2022): 216–24.

Figure 1. Co-creating The Restoration Toolbox through hands on workshops with students. Courtesy of Jugaadopolis.

Aishwarya Tipnis

Mind the Gap

Experimenting with Circularity in Built Environment through The Restoration Toolbox

Introduction

Urban Indian cities find themselves at a unique crossroads of urbanization, climate change and sustainable living. India's urban population is estimated to be 400 million by 2030, with 40 percent living in cities. India adopted the UN's Sustainable Development Goals (SDGs) in 2015 and the New Urban Agenda in 2016 with a focus on sustainable cities and human settlements for all. This commits its cities to work toward greater productivity, inclusion, sustainability and rural-urban linkages.[1] India's 2030 decarbonized policy, is aimed at increasing its nonfossil energy capacity to 500 GW and transitioning 50 percent of its energy requirements through renewable energy. At Conference of Parties UN Framework Convention on Climate Change COP 26, India announced its ambition of achieving net zero emissions by 2070. This ambition of achieving sustainable growth is being targeted through the adoption of the circular economy model, focusing on the idea of recycling and reusing.[2]

Everyday heritage helps in building a sense of pride, reinforces individual and collective identities as well as promotes intergenerational learning that not only inspires young people to explore their surroundings but also empowers them to safeguard it in the future. Metropolitan landscapes are defined by Andrew MacKenzie as an agglomeration of built environment, the system of energy and material flow, human perception and values, institutional and governance process and above all natural and ecological processes.[3] Cities are now understood as ecologies shaped by human interaction and decision-making structures that dictate its day-to-day governance. Achieving sustainability is dependent on developing programs and policies that focus on improving the qualities of place, emphasizing community engagement and partnering with voluntary sector. Research has proven that restoring, retrofitting, and reusing old buildings is a sustainable way forward and contributes to achieving a circular economy. Restoring and repurposing of everyday heritage contributes to socio-economic sustainability by encouraging new, innovative and creative uses, often strengthening social cohesion and sense of community.

Traditionally, the concepts of sustainability and conservation as we understand today, have been an integral part of the

Future Anterior
Volume XX, Numbers 1–2
Summer / Winter 2023

traditional way of life in India. Ancient scriptures such as the *Shilpa Shastra* and *Mansara* have described in great details the methods, practices, principles and rituals to be followed for the construction. The emphasis has always been on renewal, or constant care and maintenance to ensure that the cultural resources remained relevant to its society; often relying on the knowledge system of the craftsmen rather than being obsessed with the authenticity of the material fabric. However, this cultural practice is now dwindling due to the shift toward a more consumerist mindset as a result of the rapid economic growth over the last five decades. Traditional repair culture is disappearing as preference shifts toward replacement with the latest fashion trend rather than repairing existing things contributing to environmental challenges.

The idea of heritage has so far been focused on forts, places and monuments; the notion of cities as urban heritage is fairly nascent in the Indian context. The conservation of heritage buildings and spaces has largely been a top-down process, most prominent projects spearheaded by the Government agencies through specialized programs, public-private partnerships with corporates or international NGOs. It has been observed that Globalization has had a detrimental impact on the character and appearance of historic Indian cities. The state of the historic buildings and precincts in most Indian cities is dismal, plagued by issues of structural degradation as well as a host of economic and legal issues. Old buildings are being replaced with nondescript buildings not only changing the urban landscape of the city but also severely impacting pollution levels harming local communities and the planet. The concept of decarbonization is a fairly new one in India and is not understood holistically by the common man, it remains in policy documents adopted by the government and planning authorities. Therefore, the key question to answer is what role can citizens play in achieving decarbonization and building resilience toward climate change through the repairing and re-using heritage buildings? This paper explores the open-source platform of The Restoration Toolbox as a tool to empower citizens and communities in restoring buildings of everyday heritage in India.

Building the Context

As quoted by Gillian Foster:

> Circular Economy (CE) is a production and consumption process that require the minimum overall natural resources extraction and environmental impact by extending the use of materials and reducing the consumption and waste of materials and energy. The useful life of

materials is extended through transformation into new products, design for longevity, waste minimisation and recovery/reuse and redefining consumption to include sharing and services provision instead of individual ownership. CE emphasises the use of renewable non-toxic and biodegradable materials with the lowest possible life cycle impacts.[4]

Circular economy focusses on creating a system that promotes sustainability, recycling and reusing to increase the life cycle of goods. The concept of the circular economy focuses on stimulating cooperation and synergies between various actors, developing an economy of co-evolution, co-operation, co-creation, and co-ordination of actions for a common interest.[5] Repurposing projects are often informed and regulated by local policy and are affected by the levels of governance and decision-making structures.[6] It is simultaneously shaped by architectural, spatial, environmental, social contexts while being part of a continuous cultural process.

In India, the notion of built heritage for the average citizen in India is often synonymous with ancient monuments, the repair and maintenance of which is usually the responsibility of the government: restoration, refurbishment and reuse of heritage buildings appeal to a niche audience. This is primarily due to the nature of policies surrounding heritage and development. Heritage conservation has traditionally been focused on monumental heritage, the legislative protection has been provided to monuments, advocating a preservation led model. Monuments that are considered to be of national importance are protected under the Ancient Monuments Sites and Remains Act 2010, under the care of the Archaeological Survey of India (ASI). Additionally, around 100 m from each protected monument is designated as a no-development zone while 200m–300m is designed as a regulated zone under the jurisdiction of the National Monument Authority (NMA). Any new construction, rehabilitation or renovation of buildings within this zone required permission from the NMA. Citizen advocacy laid the foundations of urban heritage conservation in India in the early 1990s, with nongovernment bodies such as INTACH and other pressure groups lobbying or the preservation of nonmonumental urban heritage. The first legislation for protection of buildings of everyday heritage was adopted in Mumbai in 1995. Subsequently, several cities in India adopted the legislation to protect local heritage under the municipal law, for this purpose listed buildings are divided into three categories: Grade 1, Grade 2, and Grade 3. Depending on their value and importance, the grade determines the level of change that is permissible for each category. Every project is evaluated on a case-to-case basis by a nominated Heritage Committee. The definition of the legally classified heritage buildings is fairly conservative and narrow at the moment, and a large section of urban everyday heritage that gives character to our cities, still remains unprotected and vulnerable to replacement and redevelopment.

An analysis of the existing policies points to the lack of definitive legislative mandates or guidance for restoring, recycling or refurbishing old buildings. Even as India takes steps toward transitioning to a circular economy and sustainable development, huge gaps exist on ground between policy and practice. The integration of decarbonization in the Indian construction industry is also at a nascent stage. While steel and cement industries are recognized as major contributors to global emissions, there are hardly any policies banning them or encouraging the use of other natural or alternative materials in construction industry. This resistance from the industry is due to the existing economic ecosystems of demand and supply chains, lack of incentives for research and development or investment for complex recycling processes.

The fragmentation of power from a top-down government to multiple stakeholders at the local levels requires a collaborative governance model that brings together public, private as well as civil society organizations to address issues of economic, social and environmental aspects of urban living.[7] However, in India though theoretically there is an emphasis on participatory planning, in reality the approach to planning continues to be largely top-down. In the scenario, where Indian cities are faced with complex issues of climate change and hazardous levels of air pollution, how can citizens be empowered to repair, restore and refurbish old buildings in the absence of a robust framework for bottom-up collective actions.

Based on interviews with owners, policymakers and drawing from the experience of multiple projects undertaken by the author, it emerged that the key challenge in transitioning toward a circular economy through repurposing old buildings primarily lies in changing existing mindsets. The preference toward new build over restoration and repurposing is the key hindrance in adaptive reuse and retrofitting projects. Building on the professional experiences of the author, as well as a deep understanding of the gaps and challenges in urban heritage conservation in India; during the COVID-19 pandemic, The Restoration Toolbox was created. This free open-source tool empowers citizens and communities to restore, reuse and refurbish their own heritage buildings and spaces in a participatory way. This article discusses how this tool aims to facilitate the changing of existing mindsets of local communities toward conserving everyday heritage.

The Restoration Toolbox: An Introduction

The Restoration Toolbox (www.therestorationtoolbox.com) is built around the idea of everyday heritage, where the emphasis is not just protected and listed buildings but also those that matter to local communities. The Toolbox was developed as a direct consequence of the need generated by the COVID-19 pandemic, where for the first time, the architect or expert could not be present on site due to multiple restrictions imposed by the state during the health emergency. In the Indian context, the issue of digital parity is a very significant one given that most of the labor force and craftsmen are partially literate or illiterate and do not have access to digital tools other than smartphones. This unprecedented situation created a need to prepare user-friendly graphic resources that could be used by clients, contractors and craftsmen to DIY restoration works in the absence of an expert. As part of Jugaadopolis (a social innovation initiative that works toward making heritage relevant to young people), we conducted multiple virtual internship programs during the lockdowns through the course of the COVID-19 pandemic in 2020 and 2021. Where students and young professionals from across the country co-created manuals for the restoration of fifteen construction materials.

The project was further expanded in 2021, with the C3 Codes: Community: Creativity project on open-source technologies. Supported by Goethe Institute Mumbai, Be Fantastic and ZKM Karlshruhe. This enabled cross-disciplinary conversations with the members of the cohort expanding the idea further. Using methodologies of design thinking, the team mapped out the gaps that existed in the process of urban heritage conservation in India and brainstormed on how the online platform would innovatively respond to the challenges. Based on multiple interviews, user and market surveys and mapping exercises, interns and students developed the architecture of the platform. The platform was envisaged as a one-stop solution for heritage enthusiasts. The Restoration Toolbox eventually evolved into an open-source participatory platform, building on the ideas of inclusivity, democracy, and innovation with advice and mentorship from Platoniq Foundation, Spain. Powered by Decidim, which offers a stable, ethical, and modular architecture maintaining its code and ethical compass, while translating the model for the usage of heritage community.

The platform has three components known as processes, the first is “risk@hand,” a crowdsourced map where interested citizens can contribute a building or space they may feel is at risk. This can be done with the help of a questionnaire/checklist that helps a lay person assess the risk to a chosen building, which can be subsequently added to the building at risk map. Listing this on the platform aims at generating awareness

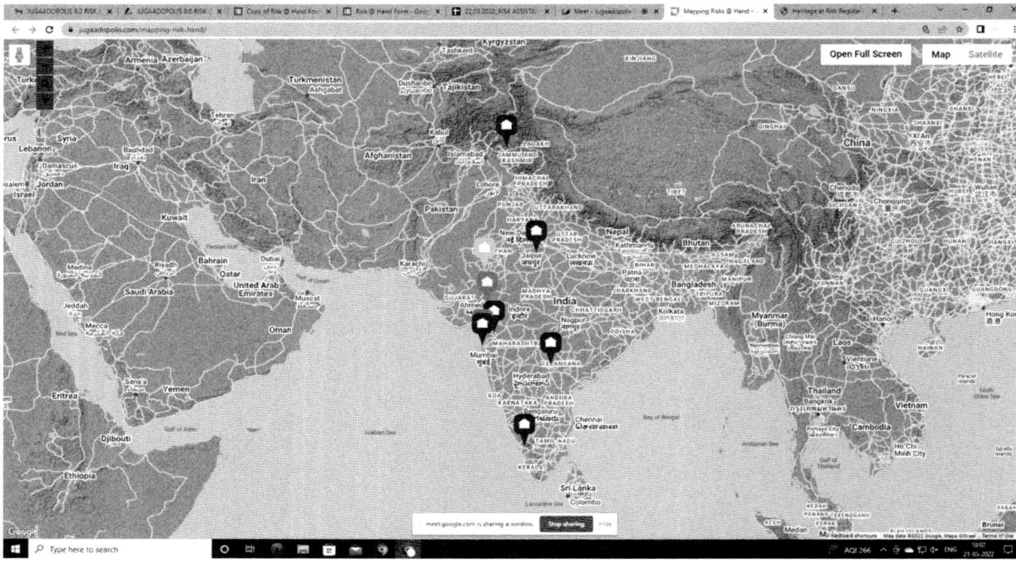

Figure 2. Screenshot of the co-created map of buildings at Risk on The Restoration Toolbox.

and creating an opportunity for recycling and reusing these buildings. The second process is a collaborative space called "build a campaign," where like-minded individuals or citizens can come together to create campaigns to save buildings that may have been flagged as being at risk. The third process is the toolbox itself, which includes a space for expert consultation for anyone seeking advice from an expert signed up on the platform, in addition to this it has the material manuals library that can be accessed and used free of cost by anyone interested in the process. The toolbox process is supported by a crowdsourced resource map of material suppliers, craftsmen, and experts, which can act like an online directory for anyone looking to implementing their heritage projects.

In 2022, the Restoration Toolbox was selected as one of the eight most innovative ideas in international cultural relations by European Spaces of Culture by European National Institutes of Culture (EUNIC). As part of the project, our aim was to make the platform accessible to the direct communities of professionals, craftsmen, policymakers, students, and entrepreneurs. This enables them to make choices in co-creating a sustainable future in the Indian context. The concept was co-created as an Indo-European project; hence we recognize that many global societies face similar challenges and even though the causes may differ, the platform possesses the ability to be replicated and adapted in other contexts as well. Through the duration of the project multiple workshops were conducted with diverse communities of students, municipalities, policymakers, heritage activists, and experts. The insights from each of the workshops have further strengthened the idea of how the tool can help in battling existing mindsets and popularizing repair and restoration as the first option.

Battling Existing Mindsets

Traditionally Indian society imbibed principles of circularity in their way of life, most things were passed on from one generation to the next. Repair was preferred to replacement; things were cared for since skilled workers were abundant and easy to find. However, post-independence there was a greater emphasis laid on industry, industrialization was promoted as the image of modernity. In the postcolonial society, traditional ideas were strategically shunned for Western ideas of a good life. Socially, traditional and old also began to be associated with the idea of regressive, while new communicated modernity. The aspirations of this post-independence society, saw the emergence of a new middle class, that adopted the idea of consumerism. This mindset privileged preference for mass produced cheap goods over artisanal, crafts-based goods. This idea further exploded with the liberalization of the Indian economy in 1990. This consumerist mindset of discarding old and getting new, translated in the urban fabric in the form of large-scale real estate development, heritage areas within both urban and rural areas were redeveloped to meet the idea of new India.

Analysis of the feedback through questionnaires and group discussions, the following emerged as the three prominent stereotypes and mindsets that required battling to popularize the idea of restoration, repurposing and repair of everyday heritage.

Mindset 1: Restoration Is a Cumbersome Process

Restoring the historic fabric is considered cumbersome, primarily due to the lack of skilled workforce, and technical knowledge as well as turnaround time for the project. Most owners shy away from undertaking a restoration project due to the complexity of the process. The legislation around listing of buildings of heritage values of cities is fairly conservative, which usually promotes maintaining status quo while discouraging any changes whatsoever. Additionally, the process for securing planning permissions for listed buildings is quite bureaucratic and cumbersome, sometimes taking up to 12–18 months which ends up frustrating most owners. The information around the process of repair and restoration of heritage buildings is mostly limited to academic circles, the lack of access to simple user-friendly resources and initiative from the local authorities or municipalities further discourages owners.

This situation can be illustrated by the case of the Seth Ram Lal Khemka Haveli, a Grade II listed *haveli* (mansion house) within the walled city of Delhi (*Shahjahanabad*). As the first project recognized as a pioneering example of restoration and retrofit design in Delhi, this restoration of a privately

Figure 3. Restoring and recycling the original timber windows at the Verdun House Mussoorie, India. Courtesy of Jugaadopolis.

owned listed building in Delhi took eight years to complete due to the lack of clarity on how regular citizens could restore everyday heritage. The primary challenge of this project was finding traditional materials and craftsmen who knew how to work with them. Through our project, young people and students were encouraged to dirty their hands and learn traditional construction methodologies and details of its restoration project were regularly shared on the project blog to inspire other people to restore their own buildings.

A key observation is the lack of awareness among stakeholders about how to recycle, refurbish or retrofit heritage buildings. Building on this experience, through the Restoration Toolbox our idea was to prepare these user-friendly graphic material manuals which could be used by owners and contractors. These manuals enabled the process of decision making, spelling out the materials, their defects, repair techniques and methods in a nontechnical way. The feedback from the stakeholder workshops on the manuals has been deeply encouraging and we will be building the library further in the next phase and make it accessible to more communities.

Mindset 2: Old Is Not Fashionable

The concepts of decarbonization, circular economy, net zero emissions are too complex for the average citizen in India. Culturally, customs and rituals play a significant role in shaping the mindset of a society. Religious and caste-based biases and prejudices also impact the decision-making processes. Social conditioning, community, and social standing are often deciding factors in the fate of historic buildings and artifacts. Currently recycling and reusing historic buildings and materials is practiced in niche sections of society, which are environmentally sensitive. For example, in the case of restoring an unlisted 1940s Art Deco Bungalow in New Delhi, the primary bottleneck was convincing the client to repair rather than replace. The benefits of restoring, repairing the historic material eventually appealed to the clients due to its cost effectiveness.

During the workshops with stakeholders, several participants expressed inhibitions around the idea of recycling, reusing, and repairing old buildings. Superstitions around the antecedents or past ownership of heritage buildings and places, legends of presence of ghosts and spirits are also seen as barriers in the adaptive reuse processes. There are also inhibitions around pre-owned vintage pieces of furniture or fixtures, beliefs about curses, good or bad omens transferring to the new owner. Successful implementation of circular economy requires further awareness building, including overcoming class and caste biases, which are fairly nuanced in the Indian society. The Restoration Toolbox creates a space for exchange of information about old buildings and artefacts within a community of heritage enthusiasts and an expert service provided through The Restoration Shop, which is an enterprise brings together craftsmen, designers, and end-users of upcycled components of heritage buildings and furniture.

Mindset 3: Restoration Is Expensive Proposition

In the current neoliberal political economy, it is hard to imagine a scenario where community benefit would be privileged over economic benefit. The nexus of politicians, real estate developers and policymakers ensure that the built heritage is often marginalized given the sky rocketing land values of these buildings. With conservative heritage policies and almost no incentives or access to public funding for heritage conservation; for most unlisted buildings to survive into the future, they need to remain relevant to contemporary times. At the moment, the building regulations do not prescribe any guidelines on restoration or reuse of existing buildings, marginalizing the concept of retrofit design in comparison to redevelopment and new construction. The lack of cohesive vision of the stakeholders as well as unavailability of relevant expert advice often leads to communities deciding in favor of redevelopment rather than restoration or repurposing.

The key idea for restoration of unlisted building is usually rooted in the emotional attachment the owners feel to their respective properties. Most projects are often constrained by the budget and thus principles of circularity, restoration, recycling and reusing are often employed to make the project

Figure 4. Stakeholder engagement workshop as part of the European Spaces of Culture 2023.

economically feasible are highly relevant. The Restoration Toolbox attempts to bridge this gap by providing access to funding through innovative funding mechanisms such as crowdfunding. The digital platform is physically supported by the Restoration Clinic, a community of craftsmen, artisans, students and professionals that provides pro bono services to help owners restore their heritage properties by themselves. As a pilot project, on the team is working on a 180-year-old unlisted heritage bungalow in Mussoorie. This project will not only build capacity of the craftsmen but also train students and young professionals in the act of restoration while reinforcing a sense of pride in the owner. Skills and capacity building is therefore a key objective for the sustenance of any adaptive reuse project.[8] The Restoration Toolbox incorporates a training and capacity building programe that trains students and youth through hands on workshop on traditional construction methodology.

Recommendations

In conclusion, decarbonization through material circularity can also be achieved through a two-pronged process: first, popularizing the idea of adaptive reuse, recycling, and retrofitting buildings through awareness building programs; second, these need to be supported by a policy environment that encourages material circularity. Urban heritage is a common resource to be shared, enjoyed and maintained collectively by the community. Existing buildings stock must be regarded not merely as a material issue, but also as an important component that makes the city itself into a source of new developments, prompted by the need for reduction of natural resource consumption, energy use and emission as well as impact on buildings from climate change. Cities must strive to achieve livability and must create a governance model that supports the civil ecology of participatory democracy. Participatory heritage conservation that is initiated at the grass root level, supported and powered by ethical open-source technology could possibly be the way forward toward empowering citizens. Such ideologies work toward creating sustainable communities while adopting systems of circularity.

The Restoration Toolbox aims builds on these design principles, where through a process of collaboration and co-design where citizens and communities play a key part in designing their own living environments.

Biography

Aishwarya Tipnis is an award-winning architect, educator, and heritage conservationist based in New Delhi. She works at the intersection of architecture, urbanism, and heritage conservation. In 2016, her work was recognized by the UNESCO Award for Heritage Conservation in the Asia-Pacific Region and in 2018 she was conferred Chevalier Des Arts et Des Lettre (Knight of the Arts and Letters) by the Government of France for her outstanding commitment to preservation of French Heritage in India. She is a published author and currently visiting faculty at the School of Planning and Architecture, New Delhi.

Notes

1 "New Urban Agenda," Habitat III, 2016, http://habitat3.org/documents-and-archive/; "SDG India Index and Dashboard | iTech Mission," Government of India, 2020, https://sdgindiaindex.niti.gov.in/#/.

2 Gloria Dickle, "COP27: India Lays out Plan for Long-Term Decarbonization," Reuters, November 14, 2022. https://www.reuters.com/business/cop/cop27-india-lays-out-plan-long-term-decarbonization-2022-11-14/.

3 Andrew MacKenzie, *Understanding Metropolitan Landscapes* (London: Routledge, 2020).

4 Gillian Foster, "Circular Economy Strategies for Adaptive Reuse of Cultural Heritage Buildings to Reduce Environmental Impacts," *Resources, Conservation and Recycling* 152 (January): 104507, https://doi.org/10.1016/j.resconrec.2019.104507.

5 Foster, "Circular Economy."

6 Bie Plevoets and Koenraad Van Cleempoel, *Adaptive Reuse of the Built Heritage: Concepts and Cases of an Emerging Discipline* (London: Routledge, 2019.

7 Aylin Orbasli and Marcel Vellinga, *Architectural Regeneration* (Hoboken, NJ: Wiley & Sons, 2020).

8 "Europe Goes Circular—Outlining the Implementation of a Circular Economy in the European Area, Dutch Council for the Environment and Infrastructure (Rli), 2017, https://www.rli.nl/sites/default/files/rli_eu_goes_circular_-_eeac_working_group_on_circular_economy_def_1.pdf.

Book Review
Lola Ben-Alon

Beit Zaman: The Old and Forgotten

Luciana Carvalho
IFAO's Printing House, 2023

> Photography is inescapably a memorial art. It selects, out of the flow of time, a moment to be preserved, with the moments before and after falling away like sheer cliffs. . . . I suggested that it is about retention. . . . But when the photograph outlives the body—when people die, scenes change, trees grow or are chopped down—it becomes a memorial. And when the thing photographed is a work of art or architecture that has been destroyed, this effect is amplified even further; that photograph becomes a memorial to a memory.
>
> —Teju Cole, in *Known and Strange Things: Essays* (2016)[1]

Beit Zaman: The Old and Forgotten presents a photography memorial. Translating into English as "House of Time," *Bait Zaman* invites the reader to dive into the *time memories* behind and beyond preservation efforts and explores how, in documenting historic structures and ways of living, photography may introduce new values and meaning. The book itself is structured as a visual photo-storytelling artifact with short textual descriptions and prompts, sharing personal stories and cultural relationships between matter, tradition, time, and the means of connecting with one's identity and heritage through architectural space. The stories transport the viewer into the bustling village—and so called silent desert sceneries—of Upper Egypt's historical heritage urbanism.

In an unapologetic realism of patina and decay, the cities of Naqada, Qift, and Qus are portrayed through their architecture and heritage that is often overlooked and at risk of destruction in the twenty-first century. Photographs, words, dust, houses; the tangible structures documented in this work are seasoned with intangible values, habits, and daily routines. Highlighted throughout the book are various modern interventions of paint enhancements, new plaster applications, fragments, and structure pieces, resulting in a patchwork of new and old materials and the informalities of localized reuse practices. The villages of the Upper Egypt region are depicted in their materiality variance: from clay plasters, to sun-dried bricks, thatch and date tree palms. A dynamic blend of old and new invites the viewer, perhaps, to sense the aromatic sensation of what was ruined, but also simultaneously embody the human effort, seamless blend with nature, and anthropological fusion of traditional heritage with modern life.

Through its case studies, the book unveils a series of intimate narratives. Woven into the fabric of the buildings in North Egypt, these narratives encourage readers to reevaluate their perceptions of decay and the inherent value of cultural preservation. In one of the documented projects, perched atop an older Christian building, was once a home to pigeons and a repository of a baptism bowl with reputed healing powers, now stands as a testament to the passage of time and the evolution of its purpose. In another image, a wooden bridge, connecting a pair of two-story mudbrick buildings in the city of Qus, is photographed, depicting a nonlinear material transition. And, in a home nestled within earthen bricks, the *galabeya* is contemplated for its material culture narrative, as a symbol of cultural identity within the Egyptian society: "'Do you want the sleeve long or short? Do you want it to reach your ankle or your foot? What about pockets? And the collar?'—Am Amgad asks Christian and Muslim clients bringing fabric for a galabeya." A fabric for wearing galabeyas is shown here to speak on not only the status of the wearer but also the mood of the day. In an adjacent room, documentation depicts photographs of family members, questioning: "photos of family members were proudly hung / their important portraits gracing the room / who were these men of such distinction?"

Traveling through Naqada, Qift and Qus in the Qena governorate, the Beit Zaman documentation project aims to fill in a gap: although many travelers visited Egypt in the nineteenth century, they did not record the "ordinary" buildings around them—yet this is the Egyptian architecture and heritage most at risk of destruction in the twenty-first century and in the face of climate change.[2] The authors emphasize the human hand as an agent in the historical iterative changes and formations within buildings, showing walls added with layers of human crafted plasters and paints, and ruins of walls revealing clay pottery infills. These buildings emerge through a spatial awareness of structural change—edited and adjusted. The human hand remains inherent to their making, forming patches of matter that come together in an intuitively engineered order, very much like craft, like pottery. "Consider a potter throwing a vessel on the wheel. . . . What is it that guides the dexterous positioning of the potter's hands and decides upon the precise amount of forward or downward pressure necessary for centering a lump of clay on the wheel? How do the potter's fingers come to know the precise force of the appropriate grip? What makes these questions even more fascinating is the ease by which the phenomena which they describe are accomplished. Yet underlying the effortless manner in which the potter's hand reaches for and gradually shapes the wet clay is a whole set of conceptual challenges to some of our most deeply entrenched assumptions about what it means to be a human agent."[3]

As a visual narrative project, this manuscript aims to speak, so it seems, to both a general public and researcher audience, while making sense of the merge of preservation specification and architectural observations, with localized stories and the everyday life. Through their social media accounts, the authors provide additional information, words of inspirations, poems, consultations, answers to inquiries, and conversations with the public. They share that, in addition to their *Beit Zaman* documentation photography, archives hold numerous images of Egypt from the nineteenth, twentieth, and twenty-first centuries—that should be paired up with modern replicates. Through collaborative efforts, the authors hope that these photographs will become "a lot more than mere snapshots—but rather be transformed into a tapestry of knowledge and to enrich the interpretation and understanding of Upper Egypt's historical urban heritage."

The authors of this book project engage in field investigations, interviews, and deep archival analysis of the stories embedded within the photographical capturing of historic Egypt. They do so in order to provide readers with a deeper understanding of the importance of preserving and appreciating cultural heritage in parallel to the ordinary built environment. It is through the eyes of the authors that the viewers are invited to unveil and remember forgotten buildings. The potency of ruins through the authors' eyes encapsulates the melding of human endeavor and nature's transformative forces.

Through this interdisciplinary discourse that enmeshes photography, design, and anthropology, books such as *Beit Zaman: The Old and Forgotten* may contextualize documentation within forms of photographic journals or diaries. Navigating challenges posed by arid environments, varying lighting conditions, and the need to maintain authenticity in post-production processes, the technicalities of such representation efforts may deepen beyond the surface of architecture and tangibility to allow readers to capture the essence of cultural memory and the urgency of preserving authenticity.

Biography
Lola Ben-Alon is a material designer, engineer, and curator. She is an Assistant Professor at Columbia GSAPP, where she directs the Natural Materials Lab and the Building Technology curriculum. She specializes in earth- and bio-based building materials, their life cycles, supply chains, fabrication techniques, and policy. Ben-Alon received her PhD from the School of Architecture at Carnegie Mellon University, and she holds a BS in Structural Engineering and MS in Construction Management from the Technion. Her work has been exhibited at the Venice Biennial, Indian Ceramics Triennial, Tallinn Architecture Biennale, Craft Contemporary Museum in Los Angeles, the Center for Mediterranean Architecture in Greece, 1014 Space for Ideas in NYC, and Tel-Aviv Museum of Art. Her scholarly work has been published in peer-reviewed academic journals such as *Construction and Building Materials*, *Building and Environment*, *Journal of Green Building*, and *Automation in Construction*, as well as reviewed in design magazines such as *Metropolis*, *The Architect's Newspaper*, and *Dezeen*. Ben-Alon is the recipient of awards including the Architectural League of New York Prize, the Future Manufacturing grant by the

National Science Foundation, and the NSF Innovation Corps grant. Ben-Alon serves on the board of ACSA's Technology | Architecture + Design, and Elsevier's Renewable and Sustainable Energy Reviews.

Notes

[1] Teju Cole, *Known and Strange Things: Essays* (Random House, 2016), 197.

[2] Hossam Ismael, Mohamed Abdel-Motamed, and Heba Ghaly, "Climate change and its impacts on selected archeological sites in Egypt," in *Hydroclimatic Extremes in the Middle East and North Africa* (Elsevier, 2024), 275–298.

[3] Lambros Malafouris, "At the Potter's Wheel: An Argument for Material Agency," in *Material Agency: Towards a Non-Anthropocentric Approach,* ed. Carl Knappett and Lambros Malafouris, 19–36 (Springer, 2008), 19.

Book Review
Kathryn Rogers Merlino

Climate Inheritance

Rania Ghosn and El Hadi Jazairy / Design Earth
Actar Publishers, 2023

World Heritage Sites invoke images of globally significant places that embody the highest level of human endeavors and represent some of the most visited sites on the planet. With the ever-growing destructive impact of climate change and the massification of tourism, preserving World Heritage Sites has become increasingly challenging. World Heritage sites were established in 1978 by the United Nations Educational, Scientific and Cultural Organization (UNESCO) to identify and protect places of outstanding universal value. Since then, the primary focus of these sites has been the conservation of cultural heritage, diversity, and maintenance of authenticity, along with the prevention of deterioration. However, climate change impacts from the frequency and intensity of extreme weather events, rising sea levels, and shifting climate zones pose direct threats to cultural heritage and present new challenges five decades later. Coastal sites are particularly vulnerable, subject to erosion and flooding, while temperature extremes and fluctuations in humidity accelerate the deterioration of historic materials and promote mold growth. Cultural landscapes' visual and environmental contexts are altered, and resource constraints and the need for adaptation and mitigation strategies complicate preservation efforts. Striking a balance between maintaining authenticity, implementing necessary modifications, and documenting and researching sites before irreversible changes occur requires a comprehensive, multidisciplinary approach involving collaboration among preservationists, scientists, policymakers, and local communities. Climate change is also recognized as a "threat multiplier," amplifying political and environmental threats that drive migration and potential conflict. While initially seen as environmental, the social consequences are inseparable and contribute to impact disparities, including extractive capitalism, mass consumption, and governance failures. Those most affected are often the least culpable, fueling the climate justice movement and posing a growing source of conflict, especially with the increasing number of climate refugees. Within these global challenges, questions arise about the priorities for World Heritage to progress in climate mitigation, adaptation, communication, and action.

Not quite as a preservationist nor as designer, the speculative design firm Design Earth confronts these current anthropogenic challenges in heritage conservation in their new

Future Anterior
Volume XX, Numbers 1–2
Summer / Winter 2023

publication, *Climate Inheritance*. Established in 2010 by Rania Ghosn and El Hadi Jazairy, Design Earth is a research practice that employs provocative architectural projects as a medium to bring attention to and raise awareness about the climate crisis. Their work critically examines the relationships between human activities, technology, and the Earth's systems. Inspired by climate urgencies, design curiosity, and necropolitics, the book *Climate Inheritance* challenges conventional institutional conservation systems and proposes alternative scenarios for preserving heritage.

In essence, the book confronts the dichotomy of disaster and heritage, change and stabilization. The book begins with exploring the aftermath of the unprecedented floods that submerged Venice under six feet of water in 1966. In the wake of the widespread devastation, coupled with the social upheaval of the decade, Italy saw a significant surge in initiatives dedicated to preserving its cultural heritage. Groups emerged, such as Italia Nostre, founded by Italian intellectuals, artists, and scholars concerned about the threats posed to Italy's historical and artistic treasures by urbanization, industrialization, and other forms of development. In contrast, alternative movements such as Architettura Radicale and the establishment of collectives like Superstudio emerged as subversive and experimental architectural activists who sought to challenge and break away from established norms in architecture and preservation.[1] Superstudio was an avant-garde architectural and design collective based in Florence and founded in 1966 post-flood by a group of young architects, including Adolfo Natalini and Cristiano Toraldo di Francia. They were known for their conceptual and experimental approach to architecture and design and were critical of traditional design and conservation theory. Rather, they explored utopian and dystopian visions, questioning the role of architecture in society and its relationship with technology, politics, and the environment. To combat the stagnant decay inherent in preservation politics concerning history and architecture, Superstudio embraced the inventive potential of disaster. They advocated for intentionally dismantling and cleansing outdated practices to pave the way for fresh possibilities. The concept of salvage introduced a suspended moment, transforming disasters into opportunities for experimentation and exploring novel ways to shape forms through accumulation.[2] This notion finds resonance in an essay by Lucia Allais (found at the conclusion of "Climate Inheritance"). Allais translates Superstudio's project, "Disaster as Experiment," which strategically challenges the iconic status of six Italian cities by proposing absurd yet specific strategies that subvert preservation norms and draw from historical disasters.[3] These proposals present alternative and imaginative outcomes in a provocative way that is directly subversive to the existing conditions of architecture under capitalism and capitalize on the power of the image rather than the place in the image itself. Inspired by these movements that call for the metonymic deconstruction of heritage as an image, Design Earth "invokes disaster logic to counter the absurdity of conservation politics, which, through the repeated failures of the UN Climate Change Conferences, have put the world on a "highway to climate hell," and ultimately suggest a form of anarchy in asking "What the hell matters in the world?"[4]

Arising from earlier explorations of alternative futures, pivotal questions emerge in the introduction regarding the future of preservation in the aftermath of climate disasters. The book advocates for profoundly reconsidering heritage in a time overshadowed by uncertainties, contemplating collapse and extinction. It proposes a shift toward the concept of "inheritance" rather than "heritage," therefore provincializing the universality of heritage and the global nature of climate change. Inheritance positions destruction within the intricate web of the world's complexities. It pushes the concept beyond the precedents of heritage, redirecting attention to the future implications of inheritance. The book then presents ten UNESCO World Heritage Sites envisioned as alternative speculative futures that counter traditional understanding of heritage. Despite the assumption that these sites are universally valued and protected, they are portrayed with a vulnerability only climate disasters can impart. Through a spatial reimagining process, each site, typically detached from its surroundings, is creatively reconnected with its geological substrate, social constructs, and political and ecological contexts. These fantastical sectional and yet two-dimensional representations of the sites' geological investigations and ecological overlays result in speculative futures. They are coupled with short narratives that integrate histories, ecological challenges, socially constructed catastrophes, and impending climate effects on each site, encompassing each site's pervasive climate risks, including rising sea levels, air pollution, habitat extinction, extreme weather, melting glaciers, material degradation, massive tourism, and the displacement of communities and cultural artifacts.

The visual narratives showcased in *Climate Inheritance* prompt contemplation of alternative futures and reparative solutions of global heritage through sites from Easter Island to the Venetian Lagoon to the Ilulissat Icefjord. Grounded in thorough research on necropolitics, histories of destruction, industrial crimes, and dispossession, the book advocates for a critical reexamination of heritage sites undergoing irreversible transformations. Through "paper architecture" (to distinguish it from design propositions), the case study chapters present a protestation of institutional preservation and a resounding call to climate action through some of the most iconic images known to us. Each chapter's graphics require patient study, interpretation, and curiosity. What heritage—and representation—means to one person is not the same to the next; such is the nature of the palimpsest presented in each of the collage drawings in *Climate Inheritance*. The speculative graphic forms of architectural representation begin to leverage symbolism as an architectural element, fostering recursive thinking to engage—or even provoke change—in media warfare against global ecological destruction.

The book raises a critical question: What *is* heritage in a post-pandemic, anthropogenically challenged era? What should preservation be when the earth is facing a crisis of impermanence within the context of global catastrophe, marked by the remnants of extractivism, racism, and settler colonialism? Drawing inspiration from early conservation movements and the endorsement of the World Heritage Convention more than fifty years ago, *Climate Heritage* identifies the appeal of globally recognized heritage sites as captivating narratives. As iconic images, they are reimagined, particularly when shadowed by global destruction. They allow us to contemplate World Heritage, our planet, and our cultural legacy, given the looming presence of climate disasters, extensive destruction, and the omnipresence of mass media in the Anthropocene era. Climate Inheritance urges a collective understanding of heritage beyond individual perspectives, challenging preconceptions, and envisioning a future where innovative approaches redefine our relationship with the past in the face of an ever-changing future.

Biography
Kathryn Rogers Merlino is Associate Professor of Architecture in the College of Built Environments at the University of Washington. She is the founder and Director of the Center for Preservation and Adaptive Reuse (CPAR), is an adjunct in the Department of Landscape Architecture and the Jackson School, and currently holds the Scan Design Endowed Chair in the College of Built Environments. Her research, projects and teaching focus on reducing resource depletion and embodied carbon by adapting existing and historic buildings, especially those promoting environmental justice and social equity. Her book *Building Reuse: Sustainability, Preservation and The Value of Design* (UW Press, 2018; paperback ed. 2021) argues that preserving and adaptively reusing buildings through high-performance retrofitting is essential for environmental sustainability, and existing structures should be considered artifacts of extracted materials and embodied carbon. She also calls for an emphasis of preservation and adaptive reuse design in architectural education, grounded in an ecological framework, so future designers are equipped to adapt existing buildings into sustainable, repairable, and beautiful places.

Notes

[1] William Menking, "Superstudio as Super-Office: The Labour of Radical Design," in *Architectural Design* 89, no. 4 (July–August 2019): 14–21. Special Issue: "Reimagining the AvantGuarde: Revisiting the Architecture of the 1960s and 1970s."

[2] Ross K. Elfline, "Superstudio and the Refusal to Work," *Design and Culture* 8, no. 1 (2016): 55–77.

[3] Lucia Allais, "Disaster as Experiment: Superstudio's Radical Preservation," *Climate Inheritance* (Actar Publishing, 2023), 142–45.

[4] Rania Ghosn and El Hadi Jazairy, *Climate Inheritance* (Actar Publishing, 2023), 12.

Book Review
John H. Stubbs

Values in Cities: Urban Heritage in Twentieth-Century Australia

James Lesh
Routledge, 2023

Well-researched, logically organized, and finely written, James Lesh's *Values in Cities* offers the first detailed history of architectural heritage conservation in Australia. Using an historiographical approach, Dr. James Lesh, urban historian and lecturer in Cultural Heritage and Museum Studies at Deakin University in Melbourne, presents in a rich and engaging way the progress of the heritage conservation ethos in Australia, primarily in the twentieth century. The focus of the book is on Australia's capital cities during the twentieth century since, as Lesh states, "the history of the twentieth-century city might be conceived of as, at once, a product of development and of conservation." *Values in Cities* is the sixth in a series within the Routledge Advances in Urban History series.

The subject addressed here—the valuing of heritage for conservation purposes—has come to be of central importance both in Australia and elsewhere. Chapter 1 of *Values in Cities* provides both crucial and compelling context for how, in the third quarter of the twentieth century, Australia assessed its conservation capacities and boldly struck out to establish an unprecedented system of theories and approaches to guiding heritage conservation practice. The book's following eight chapters tell the story starting with the formative years mainly in the early twentieth century, discussing conservation philosophy and practice roughly by decade.

Chapter 2, "Settler-Colonial Foundations, 1900s–30s," reaches back to the Australian Centenary in 1888 in Melbourne that celebrated the new country's founding years. (The famed Royal Exhibition Building is today a World Heritage Site.) The book continues through chapters 2 to 7, explaining the establishment of the Australia National Trust in the 1940s–60s; the Modern Field, 1950s–60s; the Heritage Movement and National Estate, 1970s; and Professionalism and the Burra Charter, 1970s—the latter period described by some be "a highpoint for government and public involvement in conservation." It was a period when conservation intersected with evolving environmental and aesthetic debates and when education of both the public and young professionals in the field began.

The book's earlier chapters portray how the emerging awareness and pioneering efforts by founders of the field in Australia was a remarkably enlightened affair led by several "hero conservationists." For instance, in chapter 4 Lesh states that in the 1950s most architects saw the sense in conserving exemplars of the past rather than considering them spoiled, decayed, and commercialized. Passionate radical thinker Robin Boyd railed against Australia to not be so heavy handed as American developers had been and the stressed the importance of battling the "Australian Ugliness." His seminal book of the same name was published in 1960.

Chapters 6 and 7 present the country's growing environmental awareness leading to powerful, nationally recognized forces called "green bans," which battled uncontrolled development. Green bans were hugely influential strategies for saving and rehabilitating historic buildings and conserving urban areas and cultural values in Australia. Lesh discusses the leading activists of the green ban movement and tells the stories of the great battles fought in Sydney to preserve nineteenth-century buildings in The Rocks and how in Melbourne the bans preserved Flinders Street Station, the City Baths, and Queen Victoria Market. Seen by some in the Commonwealth Government as being disruptive, anti-capital and calling out to be banned, Lesh appraises how in hindsight "the green bans themselves became an enduring symbol of radical heritage advocacy" (158). Great progress was also made in both cultural and natural heritage protection during these years in raising public awareness, new legislation, advocacy, and government commitment, with a substantial number of conservation successes to point to.

The remainder of the book addresses Australia's greatest contribution of all to contemporary cultural heritage conservation management: the carefully considered Burra Charter of 1972, which declared the country's philosophical principals and guidelines for researching, documenting, listing, and conserving its built and other cultural heritage. Chapter 7 addresses professionalism and the Burra Charter; chapter 8, frameworks, tools, and criteria; and chapter 9, changing cities and evolving values in the 1980s–90s. In these three chapters the author portrays both the people behind the overhaul of Australia's heritage management system, and how they did it. Their task was to recast prior heritage listing and conservation criteria to become something radically new—an approach that incorporates numerous additional considerations for *why* sites should be conserved and *what* should be conserved in the process. Lesh explains the lengths that authors and other shapers of the Burra Charter went to in order to research, articulate, craft, and implement a heritage conservation charter for *their* country.

Convened by the state party Australia ICOMOS, the formulation of the Burra Charter was in reaction to the monuments- and Euro-centric Venice Charter for the Restoration and Conservation of Monuments and Sites of 1964, that Australia, along with the US, Canada, and the UK had refused to sign but pledged to recognize. Lesh presents possibly the clearest-yet presentation about the Australian National Advisory Committee for UNESCO's receipt of an invitation and participation at the Second Congress of Architects and Specialists of Historic Buildings held in Venice in May 1964, the reaction of Australia's two delegates to it, and what followed. It was the genesis of the later formulation of the Burra Charter.

While not the first charter to attempt to codify criteria, principles, and procedures in architectural conservation, the creation of the Burra Charter built upon and expanded conservation theory and practice so impressively and noticeably that it represented a paradigm shift in evaluating heritage—from technology and aesthetics, the shift was to significance and underlying values. Its impact has been global. In James Lesh's detailed presentation of the story of the Burra Charter, one clearly sees how input from the other disciplines of archaeologists, geographers, town planners, museum professionals, specialist historians and landscape conservationists helped shape the Charter, both at its inception and during its several revisions, to be Australia's present effective operational guide for protecting the country's cultural heritage.

After telling of the creation of the Burra Charter the book discusses how applying the values approach to urban and suburban architectural heritage protection is much more complex than in more spacious locations such as freestanding structures and rural cultural landscapes. In comparison, the added considerations of zoning, densification, powerful economic forces, adaptive use, facadism, infill, mixing new and old, and retaining engineering and industrial areas must also be considered. Strong biases regarding urban development, sometimes having political associations, must be considered. The book addresses cases where the Charter was tested against powerful political and environmental opinions.

In explaining what distinguishes the Burra Charter, James Lesh goes into detail about what values are associated with cultural heritage conservation. There is architecture and aesthetic value and history and historic value. However, there is a plethora of other values such as scientific, social, material, spiritual, ethical, educational, recreational, economic, and visitor opportunity values, not to mention natural, biodiverse, and ecological values.

As the title implies, *Values in Cities* does not directly address heritage places elsewhere in the vastness of the continent—most notably cultural landscapes or First Nations' and First Peoples' heritage. Lesh explains how First Peoples had practically no agency within urban and architectural conservation during much of the twentieth century, though as

Australian society increased in diversity, partial ways of recognizing multicultural heritage were introduced to continue to sustain social cohesion. He explains how growth of Australia's conservation of First Nations heritage grew to intersect with the activities of authorities specializing in historic buildings while, since the 1950s, the National Advisory Committee for UNESCO, in conjunction with state museum officers, had been seeking a national survey of "aboriginal relics *in situ* in all States of Australia" (121). The long effort since, with the great help of the Burra Charter, admirably respects and addresses Australia's First Nations people today. Throughout the country, ownership of the land on which Australia's cites are built is recognized as being land of First Nations peoples, and a wide range of activities are devoted to reconciliation and national social cohesion.

The book's final two chapters also present criticisms of the Burra Charter, and the assumption that it will always be subject to revision. (Its last major revision was in 2012.) The author smoothly changes the narrative of the book from the "longitudinal" story of organized heritage protection in Australia until turn of millennium to a voice which more broadly describes how values-driven heritage protection has worked as a *modus vivendi*, especially over the past two decades. After key points in the two final chapter under the subheading Legacies, Lesh discusses aftereffects of certain conservation measures with an emphasis on the impact or effect of what occurred during a time frame or trend in the field.

While the book presents the basic players in urban conservation—the authorities, architects, planners, historians, activists, heritage enthusiasts, and property owners—there are few details on actual administration of the Charter. It does, however, offer different perspectives on heritage conservation going forward. Part of the final chapter, for instance, offers a critical view of Australia's post–Burra Charter years from a firsthand witness and practitioner, Sydney planner Helen Proudfoot, which enhances the book's objectivity. Lesh also helpfully traces the evolution of heritage education, planning principles, and heritage planning in Australia. He fairly presents the cynics view of Australian heritage conservation policy and how it has been received by pro-growth politicians, developers, and architects who probably still pointedly refer to conservationists as the "Heritage Mafia." He presents accusations by developers on the impracticalities of heritage protection, and cries of gentrification from disenfranchised stakeholders. In this respect he presents the "dichotomy of saving buildings but not the sense of community," warned by Laurajane Smith (277), also William Logan's observation on how "institutionalization of the conservation process has sapped community reaction to most conservation issues" (276). As a historian,

Lesh adds that the Charter and its compliance requirements are a great way to research things, but not so great in and of itself a way to protect things (277).

The book's concluding chapter 10, "The Past and Future of Conservation," offers a synthesis of the accomplishments of the values approach to heritage conservation as promulgated in the powerful and influential Burra Charter over the past half century. It's clear, sensible and useful tenets which have guided Australian conservation now for nearly a half century have yielded impressive results, that the country proudly presented through its long-planned hosting of the ICOMOS General Assembly Sydney in September 2023.

Values in Cities: Urban Heritage in Twentieth-Century Australia is a marvel in research, documentation, and organization of the complex story of cultural heritage conservation in Australia. James Lesh brings an impressive holistic perspective to the task and gives credit to the sources of Australian ideas and initiatives in heritage conservation where they are due. As the first detailed history of the field in Australia, *Values in Cities* should serve as an essential reference both for students, researchers, practitioners and activists in Australia and beyond who are interested in the country's inspiring conservation ethos.

Biography

John H. Stubbs is Emeritus Professor of Preservation Practice and former director of the Master of Preservation Studies program in the Tulane School of Architecture. His prior work in New York City included ten years as Associate and Assistant Director of Restoration at Beyer Blinder Belle Architects & Planners and twenty-one years as Vice President for Field Projects for the World Monuments Fund. For over two decades he also served as Associate Professor of Preservation in Columbia University's Graduate School of Architecture, Planning & Preservation. Since 2005 Stubbs has led the Time Honored Architectural Conservation Documentation Project, documenting the history, theories, and practice of architectural conservation in different parts of the world, which has thus far yielded four books. See www.conservebuilt world.com.

Book Review
Hélène Frichot

The Affect Theory Reader 2: Worldings, Tensions, Futures

Edited by Gregory J. Seigworth and Carolyn Pedwell
Duke University Press, 2023

In 2010 Melissa Gregg and Gregory Seigworth made what retrospectively turned out to be a strategic decision when they named their edited collection, *The Affect Theory Reader,* for they succeeded in securing the shimmering outlines of a newly emergent theoretical paradigm available for use.[1] Their project: to procure an inventory of shimmers. Catch them if you can. Now, thirteen years later, *The Affect Theory Reader 2* has arrived, and the well-established formula of affect: to affect and be affected, continues to offer approaches to what Derek McCormack, in the first chapter of the new reader, describes as "thinking the composition and decomposition of worlds."[2] In the marketplace of ideas, despite its very elusiveness, affect theory has held firm. With humor, when they open their new introduction, Seigworth and Pedwell describe a scene from the Netflix TV series *The Chair,* poking harmless fun at their own theoretical preoccupations. Sandra Oh's character Dr. Ji-Yoon Kim, currently occupying the position of chair of a humanities department, explains to David Duchovny, who plays himself, how the theoretical landscape has significantly shifted over the last thirty years since he was last enrolled in an institution of higher education. The first example she offers in her list of contemporary theories, which includes new materialism, eco-criticism, critical race theory, is affect theory. Now available for your entertainment too. And that's the thing about affect, it "cross-contaminates," catching you up whether you are at home watching TV or joining a political protest. It quickly becomes evident that a great deal is at stake when it comes to affect theory today, and how, at the scale of the micro-political, even before you know it, you are tending in one direction or another, but to what effect?

Affect is what emerges and fades away, resisting capture yet manifesting an impact in the aftermath of personal and political encounters: Something just happened to me. Pause. Reflect. Now, in the afterglow of whatever it was that came to pass, I say to myself: I feel happy, or I feel sad. The ascription of the personal feeling is necessarily delayed, and in any case, it is always somehow inadequate. And affect just continues generatively unfurling. Importantly, it ought not be disentangled from more diffuse affective atmospherics circulating at the scale of the body politic. The oft-cited formula of affect, affecting, and being affected, or to affect and be affected, also "to act and to be acted upon,"[3] draws attention to the fundamentally reciprocal relays of affect. An affect belongs neither to an object (of study) nor to an experiencing subject, as though it were some personal quality or property. Affect addles distinctions between subjects and objects, and in any case these nodes of sense would be better situated as *subjectiles* and *objectiles,* or quasi-subjects and quasi-objects, or any terminology that draws attention to the vibrant relational matrices animating all things. Yes, it might even be understood as a kind of animism. Other terms regularly used to describe affect include prepersonal, indeterminate, nonlinear, nondiscursive, evental (of events in their unfurling), and intense. It's easy to see why critics of affect theory such as Ruth Ley and Douglas Spencer become suspicious readers of affect theory.[4] Affect theory for them risks the evacuation of critical theory, replacing rational thought with a miasma of feelings that disable political participation.

This is why a stress on the formula of affect is important: to affect, and to be affected. It's important to place an emphasis on the reciprocity of affect, for unlike the phenomenological subject apprehending a world of phenomena and remarking on his big emotions, and how he has had to carefully bracket out the clutter of his local environment (the cries of children, distracting noises from the kitchen) to get at the essence of things, affective relays instead let stuff in. It's a veritable chorus. This is what Sara Ahmed demonstrates in *Queer Phenomenology,* when she asks pointed questions of Husserl's phenomenological method of bracketing or *epoché.*[5] It is also worth noting that her essay "Happy Objects" opens the first affect theory reader.[6] Ahmed lets in the reproductive affective labors that the phenomenologist is keen to clear out. So, affect is reciprocal, it is in motion, for Ahmed it is chance-like, dependent on encounters in real time. It has a thisness and hereness, a *haecceity,* about it. It is whatever animates relations, as Seigworth and Pedwell put it, affect is "in motion, in solution, processual, of the event."[7] Crucially, the event matters, and it does have political import.

Seigworth and Pedwell are keen to point out that affect theories must be engaged in the plural, as there are many diverging approaches to affect. Much the same was stated in the first affect theory reader too, "infinitely multiple iterations of affect and theories of affect."[8] Gregg and Seigworth nevertheless called attention to eight theoretical orientations, though like tributaries these orientations are capacious and overlapping.[9] Calling further order to this proliferation, Nigel Thrift, writing a few years before *The Affect Theory Reader,* identifies four translations of affect theory: embodied practices emerging from a phenomenological tradition; psychoanalytical approaches to drives; the philosophical Spinozan-Deleuzian orientation emphasizing relations and the capacities of a body (any body) to act; and a Darwinian evolutionary approach and something of a science of the emotions. Thrift calls affect theory "non-representational theory" and speaks of the utter ubiquity of affect at grand and ordinary scales, from the deafening roar from a sports stadium to the "mundane emotional labour of the workplace."[10] There is an inherent democracy at work in the respect expressed toward a diversity of approaches to affect, what Isabelle Stengers would call an ecology of practices, in which no practice should be assumed to be just like any other.[11] In this too, there are opportunities for learning, and for unlearning.

In *The Affect Theory Reader 2,* Seigworth and Pedwell offer coordinates to a cartography of affect, because like a tornado affect is on the move (the motion in emotion). We might attempt to track it, though we'll never catch up with it, but that's not to say we can't offer an account. They remark on the conceptual-material terrain of affect, and drawing on Spinoza, a key source for affect theorists, they call on a "modulatory schema" of "lines, planes, and bodies."[12] Affect-suffused relations orientate and disorientate, affect enables and disables. The relevant concept from Spinoza is *Conatus,* that is to say, any mode's *capacity* for life, specifically, the effort that is expressed in endeavoring to persist. Gilles Deleuze, reading Spinoza, describes the cartography of affect like this: "A thing, an animal, a person are now only definable by movements and rests, speeds and slownesses (longitude) and by affects, intensities (latitude)."[13]

Across this map, in the dynamic relay of affecting and being affected, what circulates are relations of power. M. Gail Hamner, in her chapter contribution, points out that: "Yes, affect moves, but it also sticks."[14] Depending on your encounters, and the power relations you find yourself operating within, your capacity to act is either augmented or diminished. Affect animates power relations, and where power becomes oppressive affect begins to stick, much as power coagulates. The thinker gets stuck in a rut, and at a geopolitical scale a situation gets stuck with oppressive expressions of governmentality with sometimes devastating impacts.

What does affect theory have to offer experimental preservationists beyond an excess of adjectives to describe the ineffable flow of experience? As suggested already, the passage of affect is resistant to capture, making it a particular challenge for preservationists. Though any desire to preserve the shimmering, swerving, resonating, variable intensities of affect, perhaps misses the point altogether. As Spencer argues, for those architects wishing to instrumentalize affect, the notion that affect can be applied as merely another finish retrieved from the materials library is a grave misunderstanding.[15] Architecture, it could be argued, manifests as cultural products, otherwise, why would scholars attribute heritage value to it? In her chapter, Susanna Paasonen, argues that the meanings of cultural products are always ambiguous, accommodating "multiple, possibly mutually contradicting interpretations, uses and practices, and at the very least feelings toward them can be highly mixed."[16] She argues further that we should resist any temptation to resolve tensions, to flatten differences under analytical closure. Simply, do not be tempted to do away with the mess of things.

Affect comes, affect goes, neither belonging to the experiencing subject, nor to the object or state of affairs that has impinged on the thoughts and feelings of this subject, yet affect does something to us, which means it also directs our practice. Another formula to be found in the Deleuze-Spinoza affect nexus is: to experience, to experiment. Experience and experimentation run through each other; there cannot be one without the other, and furthermore "no one knows ahead of time the affects one is capable of; it is a long affair of experimentation, requiring a lasting prudence."[17] To experience means to be part of a flux and flow of mattering-meaning, acknowledging that meaning matters, and that material things manifest signification. In the messy mix of existence, we are all engaging in processes of thinking-feeling, lodged inextricably in minor and major circulatory systems of affecting and being affected (infrastructures of affect).[18] Good and bad encounters enable or else disable our capacity to act in a world, while collectively we undertake activities of world-making and world-destroying. What are affect theories good for? This is exactly the question asked in the first affect theory reader: "So, what can affect theory do?" The argument in the first reader was that affect theory can be "turned toward all manner of political/pragmatic/performative ends."[19]

For example, Nathan Snaza, reading Toril Moi with his literary theory class, makes affect theory a pedagogical imperative, suggesting it helps us to pay attention, look at details, to think, then ask: "why this?" He works with his class to situate themselves in the colonial continuum, on stolen Powhatten land, in an institutional context constructed upon "wealth accumulated from enslaved labour,"[20] in the wake of so much death and destruction, in the wake of the Middle Passage. Despite a history of violence, he recommends a reparative reading (after Eve Kosofsky Sedgwick),[21] one that is both critical and affirmative, pleasurable and ameliorative. With his students he aspires to thinking from an "evental ontology" toward an "evental pedagogy"[22] that is suffuse with care. In the process he is after what he calls "otherwise worlding,"[23] which is an urgent call to imagine and henceforth make the world a different place.

What affect theory offers is a particular orientation relative to an environment-world, one that does not presume a privileged position looking in from the outside, but a situated position that is messed up with events as they unfurl. If you have arrived with your baggage packed with your *idées fixes,* then all you are likely to discover is a pale reflection of yourself. Snaza cites arche-theorist of affect Brian Massumi: "Don't bring your products, bring your process."[24] Leave yourself at home. Following the continuous variations of the line of affect, the researcher finds (or loses) themselves in the midst of things, obliging them to operate, as Stengers would put it, *par le milieu*. This is in fact an ethical orientation, so, affect theory can inform a practical ethics, and this is what Deleuze argues when he reads Spinoza and introduces a distinction between affections (*affectio*) and affect (*affectus*). It's easy to get carried away by the distinctions made between affect, feelings, and emotions, but rather than lingering with personal feelings and big emotions, it's what affect enables one, or two—you and me, our community—to do. What moves us.

What can we achieve together, in relation? How do we undertake our work of "otherwise worlding" in an inclusive and responsible way? There is so much to learn, if only we could hesitate long enough to listen, to pay attention. There is also much to be unlearned.

Having opened the first affect reader with a significant contribution from Ahmed, the second reader places an even more concerted emphasis on "feminist, queer, trans, critical race, and decolonial thought" as well as "Black studies scholarship."[25] Helpful cross-references might be made here to a recent edition of *Future Anterior, Learning From the Past: What Is Black Heritage?,* edited by Charlette Caldwell and Anna Gasha.[26] The editors of *The Affect Theory Reader 2,* acknowledge that in the time between the two readers much has changed. The world appears to have come undone at its seams, politically, socially, environmentally, and economically. Critical race theory, and all the areas of "study"—cultural studies, gender studies—that challenge heteronormative patriarchal white power and its combined projects of colonialism and capitalism, have become controversial in the extreme, especially in the United States, but also anywhere a marginalized group is disenfranchised, oppressed, killed. Who could have guessed that theory might become a matter of life and death, threatening the devastation of careers and local lifeworlds, upending educational opportunities and vilifying any situated position of difference. A great deal is at stake. When we venture affect theory, then a politics of affect and affective labors must be acknowledged. M. Gail Hammer is careful to situate herself as "a white woman,"[27] before analyzing what she calls tendencies toward "en*white*nement,"[28] offering a critique of the aftermath of the Enlightenment. Her citational practices lead her to respectfully engage in the important work of Sylvia Wynter, Franz Fanon, Denise Ferreira da Silva, to call out the "racial capture of affect"[29] and how it feeds the organization of unconscious bias. These are the biases we must learn to unlearn. In his chapter, Ezekiel Dixon-Román situates these biases amid the rules of algorithmic governance. In her chapter, Rizvana Bradley speaks of how "Blackness confronts a nexus of stolen pasts, of protracted presents without presence, of futurities withheld."[30] Ann Cvetkovich, likewise taking care to situate herself as a "white settler reader,"[31] argues for how affect can inform new genres of creative nonfiction that work with the material of minor feelings and everyday intimacies that push against anti-Black sentiment.

As a register of what has become a community of thinkers, if not a tradition of thought, both affect theory readers are also memorials. *The Affect Theory Reader* is dedicated to the memory of affect theorist, Eve Kosofsky Sedgwick, known for addressing shame through a reading of Silvan Tomkins. Shame shrivels us, it is defined as the most powerful of negative affects, or what might be better called a passion that pacifies us. Sedgwick is also known for her method of reparative reading, which she offers as an alternative to paranoid reading. Then, *The Affect Theory Reader 2* is dedicated to the memory of affect theorist Lauren Berlant, whose discussion of cruel optimism has no doubt haunted many scholars as they scramble about on the snakes and ladders of an academic career.[32] Immediately, in these *in memoria* we see how affect can reduce us to sad passions, disabling our capacities to act in a world, but we might also be inspired to imagine things otherwise, move ourselves to make a difference. We launch force optimistically, but institutional constraints confront us with cruel impossibilities. We stake a claim, it is overturned, we are belittled, we suffer shame. Yet we must believe in this world. Lauren Berlant has the last word in *The Affect Theory Reader 2,* writing while dying from a cancer that has invaded her body. She says: "I used to say to the politically depressed that since the world has changed during our lifetimes, it could change again, to become less bad, or even beautiful. Imagine it."[33]

Biography
Hélène Frichot is Professor of Architecture and Philosophy, Melbourne School of Design, University of Melbourne, Australia. Previously, she was Professor of Critical Studies and Gender Theory, and Director of Critical Studies in Architecture, KTH Stockholm, Sweden. She is the author of *Creative Ecologies* (2018), and *Dirty Theory* (2019). With esteemed colleagues, she has coedited *Infrastructural Love: Caring for*

our *Architectural Support Systems* (2022); *Architectural Affects After Deleuze and Guattari* (2021); *Writing Architectures* (2020); and she has recently coedited a special issue of the *Journal of Architecture: "Jennifer Bloomer: A Revisitation"* (2024).

Notes

[1] Melissa Gregg and Gregory J. Seigworth, eds., *The Affect Theory Reader* (Durham: Duke University Press, 2010).
[2] Derek P. McCormack, "The Elements of Affect Theories," *The Affect Theory Reader 2*, ed. Gregory J. Seigworth and Carolyn Pedwell (Durham: Duke University Press, 2023), 63.
[3] Melissa Gregg and Gregory J. Seigworth, "An Inventory of Shimmers," *The Affect Theory Reader,* 1.
[4] Douglas Spencer, *The Architecture of Neoliberalism: How Contemporary Architecture Became an Instrument of Compliance and Control* (London: Bloomsbury, 2016); Douglas Spencer, *Critique of Architecture: Essays on Theory, Autonomy, and Political Economy* (Basel: Birkhäuser, 2020). Ruth Leys, *The Ascent of Affect: Genealogy and Critique* (Chicago: University of Chicago Press, 2017).
[5] Sara Ahmed, *Queer Phenomenology: Orientations, Objects, Others* (Durham: Duke University Press, 2006).
[6] Sara Ahmed, "Happy Objects," *The Affect Theory Reader,* 29.
[7] Gregory J. Seigworth and Carolyn Pedwell, "Introduction: A Shimmer of Inventories," *The Affect Theory Reader 2*, 35.
[8] Gregg and Seigworth, "An Inventory of Shimmers," 4.
[9] Gregg and Seigworth, "An Inventory of Shimmers," 6–9.
[10] Nigel Thrift, *Non-Representational Theory: Space Politics, Affect* (London: Routledge, 2007), 171. An essay by Nigel Thrift was also published in *The Affect Theory Reader.* See Nigel Thrift, "Understanding the Material Practices of Glamour," *The Affect Theory Reader,* 289–308.
[11] Isabelle Stengers, "Introductory Notes on an Ecology of Practices," *Cultural Studies Review* 11, no. 1 (2005): 183–96. I also note that Stengers and her reading of A. N. Whitehead is also offered as an orientation to affect by the editors, Gregg and Seigworth, in their introduction to *The Affect Theory Reader,* 8–9. Stengers's philosophy is regularly punctuated with references to affect.
[12] Gregory J. Seigworth and Carolyn Pedwell, "Introduction: A Shimmer of Inventories," 6.
[13] Gilles Deleuze and Claire Parnet, *Dialogues II* (New York: Columbia University Press, 2007), 93.
[14] M. Gail Hamner, "Unlearning Affect," *The Affect Theory Reader 2,* 250.
[15] Spencer, *The Architecture of Neoliberalism.*
[16] Susanna Paasonen, "Ambiguous Affects: Excitements that Make the Self," *The Affect Theory Reader 2,* 96.
[17] Gilles Deleuze, *Spinoza: A Practical Philosophy* (San Francisco: City Lights Books, 1988), 125.
[18] See Hélène Frichot, "Infrastructural Affects: Challenging the Autonomy of Architecture," *Architectural Affects After Deleuze and Guattari,* ed. Marko Jobst and Hélène Frichot (London: Routledge, 2020), 10–25.
[19] Gregg and Seigworth, "An Inventory of Shimmers," 5.
[20] Nathan Snaza, "Why This? Affective Pedagogy in the Wake" *The Affect Theory Reader 2,* 262.
[21] Eve Kosofsky Sedgwick, *Touching Feeling: Affect, Pedagogy, Performativity* (Durham: Duke University Press, 2003).
[22] Snaza, "Why This?,", 268.
[23] Snaza, "Why This?," 266.
[24] Brian Massumi cited in Snaza, "Why This?, 269. Brian Massumi, "Immediation," *Politics of Affect,* 146–76 (Malden, MA: Polity, 2015), 171.
[25] Seigworth and Pedwell, "Introduction: A Shimmer of Inventories," 24.
[26] Charlette Caldwell and Anna Gasha, eds., "Learning from the Past: What Is Black Heritage?" *Future Anterior*18, no. 2 (2021): 1–27.
[27] M. Gail Hamner, "Unlearning Affect," *The Affect Theory Reader 2,* 244.
[28] Hamner, "Unlearning Affect," 241.
[29] Hamner, "Unlearning Affect," 244.
[30] Rizvana Bradley, "Too Thick Love, or Bearing the Unbearable," *The Affect Theory Reader 2,* 205.
[31] Ann Cvetkovich, "Minor Feelings and the Affective Life of Race," *The Affect Theory Reader 2,* 173.
[32] Lauren Berlant, *Cruel Optimism* (Durham: Duke University Press, 2011).
[33] Lauren Berlant, "Poisonality," *The Affect Theory Reader 2,* 460.

Submission Guidelines

Future Anterior is a peer reviewed (refereed) journal that approaches the field of historic preservation from a position of critical inquiry. A comparatively recent field of professional study, preservation often escapes direct academic challenges of its motives, goals, forms of practice and results. Future Anterior seeks contributions that ask these difficult questions from philosophical, theoretical, and critical perspectives.

Articles should be no more than 4,000 words (excluding footnotes), with up to seven illustrations. It is the responsibility of the author to secure permissions for image use and pay any reproduction fees. A brief abstract (200 words) and author biography (around 100 words), and a list of numbered image captions with credits must accompany the text. Acceptance or rejection of submissions is at the discretion of the Editorial Staff. Please do not send original materials, as submissions will not be returned.

Formatting Text: All text files should be saved as Microsoft Word or RTF format. Text and citations must be formatted in accordance with the *Chicago Manual of Style,* 18th Edition. All articles must be submitted in English, and spelling should follow American convention.

Formatting Illustrations: Images should be sent as TIFF files with a resolution of at least 300 dpi at 8" by 9" print size. Figures should be numbered clearly in the text, after the paragraph in which they are referenced. Image captions and credits must be included with submissions.

Checklist of documents required for submission:

__ Abstract (200 words)
__ Manuscript (4000 words)
__ Illustrations (7)
__ Captions for Illustrations
__ Illustration Copyright information
__ Author biography (100 words)

All submissions must be submitted electronically, via email to Future.Anterior.Journal@gmail.com

Questions about submissions can be sent to the above email address or mailed to:

Jorge Otero-Pailos
Editor, *Future Anterior*
GSAPP
400 Avery Hall
1172 Amsterdam Ave
Columbia University
New York, NY 10027

https://www.arch.columbia.edu/future-anterior

Become a *Future Anterior* Sponsor

Future Anterior is funded by grants and distributed in the spirit of making knowledge available to everyone. Donations are critical to helping us accomplish this mission. If you would like to become a sponsor, please fill out this page and mail it, with a check payable to Columbia University, to:

Future Anterior
Graduate School of Architecture, Planning, and Preservation
400 Avery Hall
1172 Amsterdam Avenue
Columbia University
New York, NY 10027

Or contribute by credit card online at:
https://arch.givenow.columbia.edu/#

All sponsors will be recognized in each issue of *Future Anterior* and receive a one-year subscription to the journal.

Please check the appropriate sponsorship level:

Individual Sponsor:	❑ begins at $100/year
Institutional Sponsor:	❑ begins at $500/year
Patron:	❑ begins at $1000/year

Name*: ______________________________

Address: ______________________________

____

City: ______________________________

State: ______________ Zip: ______________

Country: ______________________________

Institution/Office: ______________________________

E-mail: ______________________________

*please provide your name exactly as you would like it to appear in print